Leo T. Sullivan

BIRDLAND

THE JAZZ CORNER OF THE WORLD

AN ILLUSTRATED TRIBUTE, 1949–1965

Schiffer Publishing Ltd

4880 Lower Valley Road · Atglen, PA 19310

Other Schiffer Books on Related Subjects:

Copyright © 2018 by Leo T. Sullivan

Library of Congress Control Number: 2018934135

Cover design by John Cheek
Type set in Tandelle/Helvetica/Times

ISBN: 978-0-7643-5586-8
Printed in China

Published by Schiffer Publishing, Ltd.
4880 Lower Valley Road
Atglen, PA 19310
Phone: (610) 593-1777; Fax: (610) 593-2002
E-mail: Info@schifferbooks.com
Web: www.schifferbooks.com

For our complete selection of fine books on this and related subjects, please visit our website at www.schifferbooks.com. You may also write for a free catalog.

Schiffer Publishing's titles are available at special discounts for bulk purchases for sales promotions or premiums. Special editions, including personalized covers, corporate imprints, and excerpts, can be created in large quantities for special needs. For more information, contact the publisher.

We are always looking for people to write books on new and related subjects. If you have an idea for a book, please contact us at proposals@schifferbooks.com.

A special thanks to:

Marcel Fleiss for his generosity and kindness in allowing me the use of his iconic Birdland photographs, and to Cynthia Sesso of CTSIMAGES, who because of her time and effort helped bring this arrangement to fruition.

Tad Hershorn, archivist at Rutgers Institute of Jazz Studies, for use of the Birdland handbills.

Michael Cuscuna of Mosaic Records for use of Francis Wolff © Mosaic images on pages 12, 33, 34, and 45.

Andrea Derujinsky for use of Gleg Derujinsky's images on pages 17, 18, 21, 26, and 46.

Michael Rudolph for use of PoPsie Photos © Michael Randolph images on pages 1, 11, 15, 31, and 37.

James Castro for use of the © Joe Castro Collection on page 19.

Anthony and Barbara Boulanger for use of their personal photograph on page 43.

Also, to their grandson Daniel Baldassara for his assistance.

Roda Bartels for use of her personal photograph on page 20.

Cover photo and page 16 images from the Leo T. Sullivan Collection.

Back cover photo taken by William P. Gottlieb, courtesy Library of Congress, LC-GLB23-0689 DLC.

This book is dedicated to my lovely wife, Shirley, and my two children, Steven and Christine. Also, to my adorable grandchildren, Tristan, Ashton, Avery, Kingsley, and Laughlin.

CONTENTS

"We don't have any more Charlie Parkers on the scene, or Art Tatums, or Miles', or Dizzys, as far as I've seen. These guys are gone, and they haven't been replaced with anyone of that caliber. Those with style will be remembered."

Horace Silver,
jazz pianist/composer

"Most of the soloists at Birdland had to wait for Parker's next record to find out what to play next. What will they do now?"

Charles Mingus,
jazz bassist/composer

"I'll tell you a story about the swinging thing. This was the '55 band, and it was the swingingest band that I was ever on with Kenton, and I was with them for seven years.

"It was Al Porcino, and you know, some real swing players. We were in New York, and we had a night off, so Al Porcino says, 'Count Basie's band is down at Birdland. I think everyone should go down and listen to Count Basie.'

"So we all did, but not because he said it, but because we wanted to hear him. Basie's band was really hot at that time. So when we got to Birdland, across the room we noticed that Stan Kenton was in the audience.

"So the next day we get on the bus, and we're leaving New York. We're going somewhere. I don't know. To the next gig, and Al says, 'Stan! I saw you at Birdland last night. How did you like Count Basie's band?' And Stan said, 'Oh, it was great. But all they do is swing.' And the whole bus cracked up, man!"

Sam Noto,
jazz trumpeter

Many jazz clubs have opened and closed over the many years, but never has there been a venue showcasing such incredible jazz greats on a nightly basis as at the "Jazz Corner of the World," Birdland. The famed jazz citadel emerged into a million-dollar business within the first seven years of operation.

Birdland was a future aspiration for promoter Monte Kay. He was a visionary of sorts and could foresee the demise and decay of the 52nd Street scene, which was once considered the main drag of the jazz world. By the end of the 1940s, many of the 52nd Street jazz clubs had turned to girlie shows with bizarre variety acts, such as "Camille's Six Foot Sex—the King Size Glamour Girl."

The future Birdland at that time was operating as the Club Ebony, an old-time black-and-tan show joint. Just as 52nd Street had changed their entertainment format, midtown Manhattan on Broadway wasn't fairing any better. There weren't any true jazz clubs to be found.

Monte Kay, the astute promoter, and disc jockey "Symphony Sid" Torin talked in April 1948 to the operator of the Royal Roost, a fried-chicken restaurant on the corner of 47th and Broadway, persuading him to allow a bebop jam session featuring Miles Davis, Lucky Thompson, Tad Dameron, and Allen Eager. It was an overnight success, with "boppers" packing the place.

Witnessing the phenomenon that night was Ralph Watkins, who ran one of the girlie shows on 52nd Street, named "Kelly's Stable." Monte Kay and Watkins promptly obtained the lease to the Royal Roost and inaugurated a series of bop shows for the weekends, which would soon include Charlie Parker. Monte soon came up with the idea to charge an admission and install a milk bar and a peanut gallery for the younger jazz fans to sit and listen to the music. This would become the same format that Birdland would incorporate into their venue a year and a half later.

This move by Kay and Watkins didn't go unnoticed. The two operators of the Three Deuces club on 52nd Street, Sammy Kaye and Irving Alexander, quickly decided to get out of the girlie show business and take over the lease at the Club Ebony (the future home of Birdland on 1678 Broadway) and rename it the Clique. They booked the George Shearing Trio, with Oscar Pettiford on bass and Kenny Clarke on drums. They also booked Sarah Vaughan and the Buddy Rich band as competition to Kay and Symphony Sid at the Royal Roost.

The Clique was successful until the beginning of 1949, when suddenly business and enthusiasm started to wane. The club tried to hang on by booking the Oscar Pettiford All-Stars, trying to compete with Charlie Parker at the Roost, but unfortunately Bird's popularity and musicianship drew in the audiences. The Clique even tried Afro-Cuban music by hiring the Machito band, and when that didn't work they tried Charlie Barnet's band and the Lennie Tristano Sextet, but to no avail. In a last-ditch effort they abandoned jazz altogether and turned to girlie shows, featuring Sally Rand and her G-stringers, which lasted only one week, and then the club folded, leaving a dark and empty nightclub.

Monte Kay started to lose interest with the Roost and began to take a serious look at the closed Clique nightclub. By now Charlie Parker was better known as "Bird" and had become the symbol of everything modern in jazz, so Kay was positive he had come up with the right name for the reopened Clique. He would name it Birdland.

Monte Kay, née Kaplan, took a six-year lease on the basement club in partnership with his brothers Joe and Sol. The cost of the shows would be no more than $1,500 to $2,000 a week. Kay stated, "I'm going to play mainly for the kids. We won't try to sell to the general public, and we won't call the music 'bop.' We will refer to it as 'new jazz.'"

While Dizzy Gillespie was tearing it up down the street at Bop City, Birdland would present Charlie Parker, Lennie Tristano, and an unknown singer named Harry Belafonte. The opening date was set for September 8, 1949, but unfortunately when that day arrived the club had not yet been granted its liquor license. Kay, with his hands tied, took his already contracted artists to the old Onyx club on 52nd Street, which he renamed the Orchid Room.

When Birdland did finally open on December 15, 1949, the club was not under Kay's direction, and the man who dreamed up the idea was never to share in its profits. The club instead was taken over and operated by brothers Irving and Morris Levy, who had been connected with the Royal Roost operation. In Monte Kay's words, "Well, that's show biz."

CHAPTER ONE

BIRDLAND

JAZZ CORNER OF THE WORLD

Birdland, the nightclub and mecca for jazz in New York City, was named in honor of legendary jazz saxophonist Charlie "Yardbird" Parker (Bird) and opened its doors on December 15, 1949. It was located a block west of the 52nd Street scene at 1678 Broadway, and for the next fifteen years the club entertained the visiting jazz fans with double and triple bills, starting at 9:00 p.m. and usually lasting until dawn.

Birdland was hailed as the Jazz Corner of the World and was the melting pot for pure jazz at the time. It was a place where new alliances were formed and jazz musicians felt comfortable performing, sometimes even giving birth to new bands.

Birdland established itself as the one place that every jazz musician had to play, hosting Charlie Parker, Dizzy Gillespie, Bud Powell, Miles Davis, Thelonious Monk, Count Basie, John Coltrane, Art Tatum, Sarah Vaughan, Art Blakey, Horace Silver, Clifford Brown, Ella Fitzgerald, Stan Getz, Lester Young, George Shearing, Billie Holiday, Milt Jackson, Oscar Peterson, and Sonny Rollins, to name only a few.

On certain nights the audiences might have included Marilyn Monroe, Frank Sinatra, Sammy Davis Jr., Dean Martin, or Igor Stravinsky. Within the first ten years, Birdland entertained over two million jazz listeners, starting at an admission charge of 98 cents on opening night in 1949 increasing to $1.85 a person by 1959.

Birdland was a basement club, holding almost 300 people. After entering Birdland under a long canopy, you would descend the stairs to the first landing, where the ticket window and checkroom were located. After paying your admission, you descended the rest of the stairs into the club itself, entering a smoky, dimly lit room that opened up with a long bar against the left wall, where you could sit or stand while listening to the jazz entertainment. Many famous jazz musicians and celebrities would usually congregate there to gossip and catch the jazz acts.

If you preferred not to drink, there was a section to the right of the bar known as the "Bull Pen" or "Bleachers" where several rows of chairs faced the bandstand, separated from the rest of the club by a fence-like barrier. In this section, you were allowed to enjoy the nightly acts by paying only the price of admission, without having to buy a drink.

Many of the people in this section were under the drinking age and were there only to listen. It's been stated that you will never encounter a more attentive and courteous audience than the fans in the Bullpen at Birdland.

In the middle section there were ten to fifteen tables with red-and-white-checkered tablecloths, where food and drinks were served. Along the far wall there were semicircular booths whose walls were decorated with murals of famous jazz personalities, painted by the club's hatcheck girl, Diana Dale.

Dancing was not allowed, which worked out well since the bandstand (sometimes called the Birdstand) was very small, and at times, in order to accommodate a big band, the piano had to be moved off the stage to the floor.

When Birdland first opened there were caged finches hung around the walls to add to the decor, but unfortunately the birds lasted less than a month, probably due to a combination of the heavy smoke and loud music.

Birdland had a master of ceremonies named Pee Wee Marquette, who was three feet nine inches tall and notorious for mispronouncing musician's names who refused to tip him. His voice can be heard making the introductions on Art Blakey's 1954 live recording, *A Night at Birdland*.

Many live recordings were made at Birdland over the years, by such artists as Charlie Parker, George Shearing, Miles Davis, Stan Getz, Dizzy Gillespie, Bud Powell, Sarah Vaughan, Lester Young, Lennie Tristano, Count Basie, Ella Fitzgerald, Art Blakey, and John Coltrane, to name just a few.

A sound booth located near the bandstand allowed the popular DJ "Symphony Sid" Torin to broadcast a live one-hour show over WJZ radio (later to become WABC) to listeners up and down the Eastern Seaboard, as did radio announcers Bob Garrity and Hal Jackson for seven nights a week, from midnight to 6:00 a.m., until the mid-1950s.

OPPOSITE Miles Davis and John Coltrane at Birdland, October 18, 1955.

Across the street from Birdland was the Alvin Hotel, where many out-of-town
Birdland musicians would stay. Lester Young passed away in one of these rooms
after returning from Paris in 1959.

The opening of Birdland came off as scheduled on December 15, 1949, and the music was programmed to appeal to all tastes. The show was called "A Journey through Jazz," and it turned out to be just that. It covered the dixieland of the 1920s, the swing of the 1930s, the bop of the 1940s, and the new sounds of the 1950s. The featured artists were Hot Lips Page, Max Kaminisky's Dixielanders, Lester Young, Stan Getz, Charlie Parker, the Lennie Tristano Sextet, and Harry Belafonte. Disc jockey Bill Williams narrated the show, which ended up being one of the weirdest jam sessions in history. Lennie Tristano stated, "I was afraid at first that some of the Dixie fans might boo Charlie Parker, or the boppers might put down the Max Kaminsky Dixielanders. But everybody was happy."

Soon after the opening, a house band was formed featuring the talents of Al Haig on piano, Curly Russell on bass, and Max Roach on drums. The horn players rotated, so you never knew who was playing at any given time. It was hard to tell who the regular horn players were in the band because there was so much sitting in. You could hear Charlie Parker, Dizzy Gillespie, J. J. Johnson, Fats Navarro, Kenny Dorham, Miles Davis, Lucky Thompson, Milt Jackson, Sonny Stitt, and others. It seemed that every musician in modern jazz was playing at that time.

Birdland prided itself by having the ability to provide music nightly with groups of various sizes—trios, quartets, quintets, and big bands. Bands were usually hired for six nights a week, which worked out as Thursday through Wednesday, with Monday night off for jam sessions. Sidemen would usually make around $90.00 a week, and the leader would make double that amount.

The musician's dressing room was very cramped, accommodating only about four people at a time. There was a bench outside the dressing room and a bathroom nearby, which would at times be hard to access due to some musicians needing a secure and private location to feed their habit. This inconvenience would at times lead to some musicians heading to the bar, allowing them to strike up a conversation with the customers and possibly score a drink or two.

Birdland played host to many sensational female vocalist over the years, including Ella Fitzgerald, Billie Holiday, Dinah Washington, and the first female vocalist to be featured in a series of network broadcasts from a New York nightclub, Sarah Vaughan. Sarah was broadcast via WJZ and the coast-to-coast facilities of ABC, direct from the floor of Birdland.

There were some violent moments in the history of the club. In 1959, one of its founders and co-owners, and brother to Morris, Irving Levy, was stabbed to death inside the club. Also that very same year, Miles Davis was beaten and bloodied while being arrested by a policeman while having a smoke outside Birdland. Miles was later acquitted of disorderly conduct and assaulting an officer.

Birdland continued featuring live jazz until 1965, briefly flirting with a rock-and-roll policy in the spring of 1964, allowing for the first time an area for people to dance. Jazz would return in the summer, playing host to the homecoming of bebop pianist Bud Powell, who had been living in France for the last five years.

Once again in 1965, Birdland unsuccessfully tried rock and roll, ending up closing the club for good shortly thereafter. "I've had it. In the past two years, jazz musicians started to go too far out. They've lost their audience," explained manager Oscar Goodstein, a man who personally is devoted to jazz and who has helped launch the careers of many a jazz artist. "While the small groups are going too far out, big bands are outpricing themselves. I can pack the place with a big band and lose money, because the bands charge too much. Birdland's shows cost from $4,500 to as much as $10,000 a week," explains Goodstein.

In June 1964, Birdland filed a petition for bankruptcy, listing liabilities of $103,778 and assets of $7,320. Among the listed creditors were Goodstein himself at $22,490, the NLP Restaurant at $12,275, and Gerry Mulligan, who was owed $3,500 through International Talent Associates. Goodstein stated that he would lower his own salary so he could keep the fourteen-year-old operation going, but unfortunately the writing was on the wall.

According to Goodstein, another reason for closing was Broadway's high rent and general overhead, which made it impossible to support a jazz club. The Birdland club would be purchased two years later by Lloyd Price (a rock-and-roll singer), who renamed the place the Turntable.

Birdland would have a reunion of sorts, but for one night only on November 3, 1977. Both Pee Wee Marquette, the diminutive greeter and emcee, and "Symphony Sid" Torin would partake in the evening's festivities. Kicking off the show was Dexter Gordon with a group featuring Slide Hampton on trombone, Woody Shaw on trumpet, Rufus Reid on bass, and Kenny Clarke on drums.

OPPOSITE Buddy Rich and his band at Birdland, April 2, 1959.

Later on, Helen Humes took the room by storm, backed by Buddy Tate on tenor sax and pianist Barry Harris. Bebop baritone sax man Cecil Payne would also perform that evening with jazz vocalist Earl Coleman, who along with the band offered reminders of the club's musical history by playing such Parker standards as "Billie's Bounce" and "Now's the Time."

Musicians who packed the basement included Gil Evans, Don Elliott, Dick Hyman, Horace Silver, Billy Taylor, Walter Bishop Jr., Jimmy Rowles, Buck Clayton, Dick Katz, Percy and Jimmy Heath, Helen Merrill, Ted Curson, George Wein, and Randy Weston, to name a few.

There was talk that evening about interest regarding holding a Birdland night every Monday night if a tie-in with CBS could be arranged, but unfortunately it never came to fruition.

Slide Hampton, Rufus Reid, and Dexter Gordon at Birdland reunion in 1977.

Buddy DeFranco backstage in his dressing room at Birdland in 1952.

Lester Young ("Prez") sitting at a table in Birdland in 1952, warming up his horn.

Jazz pianist Joe Castro with various jazz artists at Birdland in 1957.

TOP LEFT Joe Castro, Philly Joe Jones, Cannonball Adderley. | **CENTER** Joe Castro
BOTTOM LEFT Philly Joe Jones, Joe Castro, Sam Woodyard | **TOP RIGHT** Joe Castro and Duke Ellington
BOTTOM RIGHT Joe Castro, Oscar Goodstein, and Duke Ellington at Birdland

Paul Motian and Bill Evans in New York City, in 1957. At Birdland, along with Scott LaFaro, they would record the 1960 *Birdland Sessions* album.

Sammy Davis Jr. hanging out at Birdland in 1952.

CHAPTER TWO

BIRDLAND

HEADLINERS

CHARLIE "YARDBIRD" PARKER

Charles Christopher Parker Jr. was born on August 29, 1920, in Kansas City, Kansas. Charlie first picked up the alto saxophone at the age of eleven and began to play in the high school marching band, working in local dance halls by the age of twelve. He was married at the young age of sixteen, eventually having a child, and later left for New York City by the age of twenty.

While growing up in Kansas City, Charlie got to hear many of his idols, such as Coleman Hawkins, Louis Armstrong, Ben Webster, and Lester Young.

Soon after Parker arrived in New York City, he became a member of Jay McShann's band in 1940, getting to record his first solos at that time. It was during that time that his nickname of "Yardbird" was shortened to "Bird."

In 1942, it didn't take long for Dizzy Gillespie, who was working with the Earl Hines band at this time, to convince Hines to hire Parker. They soon became close friends, later joining Billy Eckstine's band, where they were able to expand musically.

In 1944, Parker and Gillespie would form their first bebop quintet and record such classic tunes as "Salt Peanuts" and "Shaw Nuff." Later in 1945, Parker would lead a record date marketed as the "greatest jazz session ever," employing such jazz greats as Dizzy Gillespie, Miles Davis, and Max Roach and recording the songs "Now's the Time" and "Billie's Bounce."

By this time, Parker's drug addiction was catching up to him, and during an engagement with Gillespie in Los Angeles, Parker had to be confined for six months to the Camarillo state mental hospital for his drug and alcohol addiction.

Parker made his European debut at the Paris International Jazz Festival in 1949, returning later that year to New York City to record *Charlie Parker with Strings*. He would also perform at the grand opening of Birdland on December 15, 1949.

In 1950, Parker would tour Scandinavia without his quintet, opting to use local bands instead, recording such pieces as "Confirmation" and "Chi-Chi."

Upon his return to America, Parker began to suffer from his constant drug and alcohol abuse and was hospitalized for treatment of an ulcer, being told he would die if he continued drinking. Less than a year later he would lose his cabaret card, preventing him from working at any New York club for fifteen months.

When Parker got his cabaret card returned in the spring of 1953, his reputation was so damaged that club owners were hesitant to hire him. He would perform on May 15 of that year at Massey Hall in Toronto with Gillespie, Mingus, Powell, and Roach for a concert event that would come to be called "the Greatest Jazz Concert Ever."

Bebop helped Parker's reputation grow, but unfortunately his addictions would continually sidetrack his success. He was constantly broke and pawning or selling his saxophone to buy drugs and alcohol.

In 1954, he was admitted twice to Bellevue Psychiatric Hospital and even tried to take his own life twice by drinking iodine, yet he still had the fortitude to perform at many club dates.

On March 12, 1955, Charlie Parker sadly would pass away at the age of thirty-five from a ulcer attack and pneumonia while visiting the New York City apartment of his friend Baroness Pannonica "Nica" de Koenigswarter. The coroner conducting his autopsy mistakenly thought he was examining a man between fifty and sixty years of age.

• • •

Charlie Parker spent more time performing outside Birdland then he did in the nightclub named in his honor. Due to his drug and alcohol addiction, and continual personal and creative pressures, he could be unstable, unpredictable, and unreliable. One thing for certain, though—when Parker was stable and on his game, he was a force to be reckoned with, a true emotional and technical genius.

During the first three months at Birdland, Parker used a quintet consisting mainly of Red Rodney on trumpet, Al Haig on piano, Tommy Potter on bass, and Roy Haynes on drums. A few times he boosted his quintet to a sextet by adding the first and best bebop trombonist, J. J. Johnson.

The evening of June 30, 1950, was an exceptional night, even by Birdland's standard. It was broadcast live on WJZ, showcasing a quintet of bebop's top musicians with the addition of Bud Powell on piano and Art Blakey on drums. The trumpeter that evening was Fats Navarro, who sadly was in severe physical decline, having lost half his size due to illness. Navarro unfortunately would pass away seven days later from tuberculosis. He was a man whose true genius has yet to be recognized. The broadcast that evening was recorded, therefore preserving some of the finest playing and longest solos from the bebop all-stars in attendance.

Bird and strings would make their premiere performance at Birdland on July 6, 1950, to a full house. Some critics panned the concept of Charlie Parker being backed by a string section. A *DownBeat* reporter who had attended the performance that evening, wrote an article that appeared in the August 25, 1950, issue. "What artistry the Bird has shown in his work with small groups seems to dissipate when he is superimposed on a string section working over some sturdy standards. His usual light, rollicking inventiveness appears to desert him, to be replaced by a heavy-handed stodginess.

His tone becomes a flat, monotonous, squawking thing, and his work in general appears to have little relationship to what is going on around him. The contrast between standard Parker and Parker with strings is brought out sharply when he ends a set by going into a brief display of thematic material with only the rhythm section behind him. Suddenly he seems relaxed and at home. His horn is in proper juxtaposition to his accompaniment, and the Parkerian phrases flow easily and pleasantly once more."

In December 1950, after cutting short a tour of Europe, Charlie had to check himself into a Manhattan hospital with a severe ulcer condition due to his ongoing alcohol and drug consumption. After spending a week in the hospital, he snuck out one night wearing only his pajamas and hailed a cab to Birdland, where he sat at the bar drinking scotch and milk. After a few hours of drinking, the manager, Oscar Goodstein, convinced him to go back to the hospital, where he slipped back in by climbing up a fire escape, without alerting any of the hospital staff.

One Saturday night in early 1951, the Charlie Parker quintet was the featured attraction at Birdland. The club was full except for a table up front with a reserved sign on it. The Billy Taylor Trio were the opening act that night. When Parker's quintet walked onto the bandstand, trumpeter Red Rodney noticed that Igor Stravinsky was sitting at a reserved table in front of the bandstand. Rodney told Parker of Stravinsky's presence, but instead of Bird making eye contact with Stravinsky, he began to call the first tune, "KoKo," immediately breaking into the song at an extreme tempo— at over 300 beats per minute. Parker was in fine form, and when it came to his second solo chorus, he inserted a few lines from Stravinsky's "Firebird Suite," causing Stravinsky to roar with delight— pounding his glass on the table and sending his drink and contents high in the air. Parker never once looked at Stravinsky during his melodic insert, but it was obvious to the band that Stravinsky was both honored and moved by Parker's display of intuitive brilliance.

In June 1951, Charlie Parker stepped onstage at Birdland to do some guest solo work for a band led by the Afro-Cuban percussionist Machito, and was apprehended for drug possession. It would be fifteen months before Parker would grace a New York City stage again, having been stripped of his cabaret card—a license required of all persons working in New York City nightclubs. Parker was forced to go on the road with big bands and pickup rhythm sections. The card had to be renewed every two years, but ironically artists deemed unfit to perform in nightclubs could still play major theaters and concert halls, as did Billie Holiday four years prior.

Parker did try to get his cabaret card back, writing a letter to the State Liquor Authority on February 17, 1953, that read, "My right to pursue my chosen profession has been taken away, and my wife and three children, who are innocent of any wrongdoing, are suffering. I feel sure that when you examine my record and see I have made a sincere effort to become a family man and a good citizen, you will reconsider." Charlie's wife, Chan, recalled two detectives visiting Parker around this time and offering to reinstate his license in exchange for names of other junkies, but Bird wouldn't

Charlie "Yardbird" Parker at Birdland in 1952.

talk. Finally, after a long time waiting, Parker's card was reinstated on March 17, 1953. Prior to Charlie's cabaret card reinstatement, he was still allowed to sit-in at Birdland, but without remuneration.

On one particular night in 1952, the Stan Getz Quartet was performing at Birdland, and Stan was in the middle of his opening number, "You Stepped Out of a Dream," when he noticed Charlie Parker sitting on the steps at the back of the stage. All of a sudden and without notice, Charlie gets up on the bandstand, surprising Getz, who then asks Parker if he wanted to play. Parker replied, "No, I want to hear the piano player play a couple of choruses, because I don't know that tune." After the pianist, Al Haig, finished his solo, Parker took over and tore the roof off the place. Stan looks over at Don Lamond, the drummer, and said, "Jesus, I don't believe this guy."

Soon after Bird had his card reinstated and was legal to perform in New York City, Dizzy Gillespie decided to pop in and surprise Charlie, who was then working at Birdland with his quartet. Dizzy was playing down the street at Snookie's, so during a break he went over to Birdland, carrying his trumpet. After descending the staircase at Birdland, he saw that Bird was onstage in the middle of a performance, so he pulls out his trumpet while still standing in the doorway and begins to play some high-register bop licks in true Gillespie-esque fashion. Parker immediately answers Dizzy back with some burning bop licks, trading four- and eight-bar phrases and sending the audience into a screaming frenzy.

From August 26 to September 15, 1954, Charlie Parker was booked to play Birdland with strings. There were also two other attractions booked for those three weeks—Dinah Washington and the Dizzy Gillespie Orchestra. The first three nights went off without incident, but on the evening of the twenty-ninth, Charlie and Dinah were partying heavily in her dressing room—since they were both celebrating their birthdays that evening. When it finally came time for Bird to take the stage, he began to argue and quarrel with the string section, and in no time it came to a breaking point, with Charlie losing his temper and firing the entire string section, leaving the audience in complete shock. Charlie went to the bar and began drinking straight whiskeys, but since the string section was under a union contract for the entire three weeks, they followed Charlie to the bar and began to demand the wages that were due to them. Noticing the ongoing commotion was the manager, Oscar Goodstein, who told Parker that he was banned from the club.

After Parker's banishment from the club, Chet Baker was booked at Birdland. Since Parker wasn't allowed to enter the club, he would stand out in front of the club and tell customers how wonderful Chet's band was, and then, after getting chased off by the management, Parker would sneak behind the building, which was lined with trash cans, and knock on a door that opened to the dressing room. Chet Baker would open the door and let him in, and they would play chess until it was time for Chet to perform, at which time Parker would then sit alone in the room with the door ajar so he could hear the music.

The last time Parker worked at Birdland was on the weekend of March 4–5, 1955. He brought in an all-star band consisting of trumpeter Kenny Dorham, pianist Bud Powell, bassist Charles Mingus, and drummer Art Blakey. The first night went relatively well, but on the second night, Parker and Powell clashed. It was obvious that Powell had been drinking and was uncooperative, having difficulty in playing the same song as Parker. He would stop playing, turn around, and stare at the audience, and then change the tempo and key of the song. Parker tried to control the situation, at times repeatedly calling Bud by name and trying to get him to focus, but to no avail. At one point, Mingus got on the microphone and said to the audience, "Ladies and gentlemen, please don't associate me with any of this. This is not jazz. These are sick people." It didn't take long for this situation to get completely out of hand, and the inevitable occurred with Parker storming off the stage and heading for the bar, where he proceeded to get drunk. He was eventually asked to leave by Oscar Goodstein, and before he left, Parker spoke to Mingus, telling him, "Mingus, I'm going someplace pretty soon, where I'm not gonna bother anybody."

Pianist Lennie Tristano tells a story about Bud and Parker, saying, "I was sitting with Charlie Parker and some musicians at a table in Birdland when Bud Powell came by and said hello, and then, for no apparent reason, he said, 'You know, Bird, you ain't shit. You don't kill me. You ain't playing shit now.' To which Lennie replied, 'Bud, don't talk that way. Bird's your poppa.' Bird then spoke up and said, 'Lennie, don't pay any attention. I dig the way he plays.'"

Charlie Parker would never return to Birdland, and sadly, he would die seven days later on March 12, 1955, at the age of thirty-four, his death brought about by years of chronic substance abuse and neglect.

Charles Mingus put the genius and musical brilliance of Charlie Parker in context when he stated, "If Charlie Parker was a gunslinger, there'd be a whole lot of dead guys."

Charlie Parker cutting his birthday cake at Birdland on August 29, 1950.

DIZZY GILLESPIE

At Birdland in the summer of 1950 there was Bird with strings, Coleman Hawkins with his group, and Dizzy with his combo. One night Dizzy was about to get onstage when somebody discreetly hands him a bundle of joints wrapped in a rubber band. He quickly sticks them in his outside upper jacket pocket, where he keeps his handkerchief, and proceeds to get onstage and play. He starts out by playing a long number and begins to work up a sweat, so he pulls out his handkerchief and out comes this bundle of marijuana joints, falling on the stage in full view of the audience members. Luckily, a friend of Dizzy's sitting at the front table notices the mishap and taps Dizzy's shoe, alerting him to the joints on the stage. Dizzy steps in front of them and kicks them back with his heel to the pianist, who quickly picks them up. On the break the pianist gives Dizzy the bundle, and Gillespie has an idea to invite the band, Charlie Parker, and his friends at the front table to go outside and smoke the pot he had just scored. On his way out of Birdland, Dizzy notices Billie Holiday at the bar, so he invites her along as well. They all parade out of the club, up to the corner of 58th Street, and proceed to pass around the joints and get high.

During the first month of 1951, Dizzy played Birdland with a sextet consisting of John Coltrane on tenor sax, Milt Jackson on vibes, Billy Taylor on piano, Percy Heath on bass, Art Blakey on drums, and Joe Carroll on vocals. Unfortunately, when Dizzy returned to Birdland in March of that year he had to let Coltrane go because of his serious heroin addiction. Shortly afterward, Birdland would play host to an all-star quintet, which would pair Dizzy and Parker together with Bud Powell on piano, Tommy Potter on bass, and Roy Haynes of drums. Over the years this legendary evening became known as "the Summit Meeting."

Bassist and author Bill Crow tells of an incident at Birdland one night. "Whenever Pee Wee Marquette finishes announcing an attraction at Birdland, he usually walks off the bandstand leaving the microphone at the height he had adjusted it for himself, about three feet from the floor. "One night, Pee Wee announced, "And now, ladies and gentlemen, Birdland proudly presents, Dizzy Gillespie!," and walked away from the microphone. Out came Dizzy on his knees to accept the applause and announce the first tune. The microphone needed no adjustment."

During 1953 and 1954, the Dizzy Gillespie Orchestra took center stage at Birdland, working opposite Sarah Vaughan, Illinois Jacquet, Lester Young, Dinah Washington, the Bud Powell Trio, and Charlie Parker with strings. The house was jam packed nightly, with lineups down the block. Dizzy, the "King of Bebop," would delight audiences nightly with his playing, antics, gestures, and mimicry.

In 1955, the Dizzy Gillespie All-Stars, featuring the "King of Bongos," Candido, would work for many weeks at Birdland, playing opposite the Stan Getz Sextet and vocalist Al Hibbler.

In November 1956, the Dizzy Gillespie Orchestra would return to Birdland for two weeks. It would be broadcast live in hi-fi, featuring such greats as Lee Morgan on trumpet, Benny Golson on tenor sax, and Wynton Kelly on piano.

Dizzy Gillespie at Birdland on February 6, 1955.

BUD POWELL

Powell worked at Birdland regularly, playing in trios, in combos, and with various instrumentation until his arrest for heroin possession in August 1951. That arrest would again have him committed to a state psychiatric hospital and be unable to work at Birdland until February 1953. Powell had spent many long stretches in institutions during the late 1940s, suffering sometimes abusive and primitive treatment.

After Bud Powell was released from the institution in 1953, he returned to Birdland under the supervision of Oscar Goodstein—his now legal guardian and business manager. He began living in a small penthouse apartment, always under the scrutiny and supervision of Birdland manager Goodstein.

Morris Levy would have Powell sign over all of his publishing rights for any compositions he would write. The original compositions had to be written out on music manuscript paper and given to Oscar Goodstein, who would then, in turn, hand them over to Levy.

Powell would play weekly trio dates at Birdland after his release from the institution, which were broadcast over the radio and sometimes recorded onto acetate discs. At twenty-eight years old, he continued to perform at a superlative level, but by the end of 1953, his past treatments, beatings, drug and alcohol abuse, and recent work schedule at Birdland finally took their toll. It got to a point that one night between sets, Bud Powell sat down with Goodstein and told him he felt he was playing badly.

While Powell was obviously a genius, he was deteriorating gradually. With his now-uncommunicative facial stare, it became apparent how much effort and concentration it took for him to play. Some nights his playing was pure genius, and at other times he would mess up the form of the song. He had become an introvert, with the only form of communication being music.

One night at Birdland in 1955, Bud Powell was at the piano with his trio. Art Tatum was in the audience and, not known for making compliments, stated that he thought Bud had no left hand. When word got back to Bud, he took out his pocketknife, cut his left hand, bandaged it up, and went on playing the rest of the set with his self-inflicted injury. He continued to play with such virtuosity that Tatum was amazed. Powell's manager at the time, Oscar Goodstein, tried to persuade Bud not to play the next set, but Bud insisted on playing. Word has it that Art Tatum was very upset by the incident and never forgave him for it, but there have been many conflicting stories regarding Art Tatum's incident with Bud, including that after Tatum's remark about Bud having no left hand, the next set Bud sat on his right hand and played everything with his left hand. Afterward, Tatum was filled with nothing but praise for Powell.

Bud Powell Trio performing to a full house at Birdland in 1957.
The Stan Kenton Orchestra was also performing at Birdland that evening.

Actress and singer Pearl Bailey being escorted into Birdland
under the world-famous canopy for an engagement in 1950.

MORRIS LEVY

Morris Levy and Morris Primack bought the club that would become Birdland in the fall of 1949. Some sources say that Morris Levy and Monte Kay bought the lease to the club by borrowing money from Joseph "Joey the Wop" Cataldo (a well-known underworld figure) and used Primack only to apply for the liquor licence, since he had a clean record and cash on hand.

Morris was more than prepared to operate a nightclub, especially after having many years of experience working in the nightclub business, running checkrooms and darkroom concessions. He operated a lucrative business processing the photographs that the girls would take in the club, and return the finished product to the customers that very same evening.

Levy was known to have strong ties to organized crime, and he was not a person to mess with. He would pay the nightly entertainment and club expenses from the large sums of money he won from gambling, and from the proceeds of Roulette Records, of which he was the owner. He also operated one of the first integrated clubs on Broadway, helping build the careers of Bud Powell and Dizzy Gillespie and, most certainly, the reemergence of Count Basie.

One day Levy was approached by a representative from ASCAP and was told he must pay the publishing company a monthly payment for the privilege of booking live music. Levy explained, "A guy comes in from ASCAP and said he wanted money every month. I thought it was a racket guy trying to shake me down. I wanted to throw him out. And then he came back again and said he's going to sue. I said, 'Get the hell outta here.' I went to my lawyer and I said, 'What is this guy? He keeps coming down and wants money!' My lawyer said, 'He's entitled to it. By act of Congress, you have to pay to play music.' I said, 'Everybody in the world's gotta pay? That's a hell of a business. I'm gonna open up a publishing company.'" Morris formed Patricia Music and acquired rights to all the songs first performed in Birdland, including the venue's soon-to-be-famous "Lullaby of Birdland."

By 1952, Morris Levy decided he wanted to have a theme song to open up the Symphony Sid radio show on WJZ Radio, which was broadcast live from Birdland, so he gave pianist George Shearing a piece of music to record for the show. Shearing considered it and didn't like the song, so he offered to write an original song for the show. After some bartering back and forth, Shearing agreed to give Levy the publishing rights for the song he would compose, but he would keep the composer rights for himself.

For weeks, Shearing tried to come up with something, but to no avail. Suddenly one night in the middle of dinner he jumped up, went to the piano, and wrote the theme song, "Lullaby Of Birdland" in ten minutes. Shearing explains, "Actually, quite a lot of my compositions have come this way. Slow going for a week or so and then the piece comes together very rapidly." Shearing ended up recording the instrumental for the radio show and ultimately adopted it as the theme song for his quintet.

PEE WEE MARQUETTE

William Clayton "Pee Wee" Marquette was the master of ceremonies at Birdland; he was a three-foot-nine-inch-tall African American who spoke in a high-pitched voice, frequently slipping into the dialect of Montgomery, Alabama, his birthplace. He dressed in a brown-pinstripe vested suit and a floral tie, or a dark-green velvet suit with a large bow tie. On special occasions he wore a black tux with tails, or a white tuxedo coat.

Pee Wee wore one of two facial expressions as master of ceremonies: a superior, disapproving frown that indicated the importance of his office, or an exaggerated, toothy grimace that he reserved for mooching tips. Not just from customers—Pee Wee expected a gratuity from each bandleader who worked at Birdland, and since he announced the name of each musician before each set, on payday he let it be known that he expected a dollar per musician for the publicity. If you refused to tip Pee Wee, he would deliberately mispronounce your name. On one occasion, he called jazz pianist Horace Silver "Whore Ass Silber"! For this and other reasons, Pee Wee was dubbed by Lester Young as "the Half-Pint-Sized Master of Ceremonies," and the less complimentary "Half a Motherf***er"!

When Pee Wee would introduce the band he would climb onto the bandstand, pull the microphone down, and shout in his Alabama accent, "And now, laydahs and gentlemen, Birdland, the jazz cornah of the world, is proud to present, the one and onlah . . ." After naming the bandleader and musicians, he would ask for a "large round of applaw" for the band. He would then climb off the stage and tell the band, "All right now fellas, let's get right up heah! We don't want no lulls roun' heah! No lulls!"

In 1960, jazz vibraphonist Bobby Hutcherson had a legendary encounter with Pee Wee. Bobby had just traveled from California to New York City to appear at Birdland when he was approached by the diminutive Pee Wee Marquette. Here is the encounter as told by Hutcherson:

"Pee Wee walks in with this long cigar in his mouth and says, 'Who you?' And I said, 'Well, I'm Bobby Hutcherson and I'm playing with Al Grey and Billy Mitchell.' So he blew a big puff of smoke in my face and says, 'Take and pack your instrument up and get on outta here. We don't need you. We got Lionel Hampton and Milt Jackson.' So I said, 'You ain't gonna throw me outta here.' So I kept on setting up my instrument.

"Pee Wee was known, that if he didn't like you, he would mess up your name. So for the first week when he would introduce the group, he would say, 'Ladies and gentlemen, from the Jazz Corner of the World, Birdland, 52nd Street and Broadway, the Al Grey–Billy Mitchell Sextet, with Al Grey and Billy Mitchell.' Then when he got to my name, 'and Bubba Hutchkins on vibes!' And I said, 'Oh Lord!'

OPPOSITE Pee Wee Marquette, Chan Parker, and Erroll Garner at Birdland, June 15, 1950.

"So on pay night across the street at the Alvin Hotel, I was in Al Grey's room getting paid. There was a knock at the door, so I opened it. It was Pee Wee Marquette with this big cigar in his mouth, blowing smoke in my face, saying, 'Hey Poppa, you got something for me?' I knew he was waiting for some money, so I said, 'Are you kidding? Not the way you've been introducing my name!' Al Grey yells, 'Give him five dollars!' Well, in 1960, five dollars was a lot of money! So I said, 'I ain't givin' him five dollars!' 'Give him five dollars. You'll see the difference,' yells Al Grey. So I hand him five dollars, and Pee Wee says, 'Thank you, Poppa.' He slams the door and walks off.

"Well, because I gave him the five dollars, the next week Pee Wee introduces the group 'from Birdland, 52nd Street and Broadway, Al Grey, Billy Mitchell, and Bobby Hutcherson on vibes!' Al Grey turned to me and says, 'See what five dollars does? Now everybody knows what your name is!'"

Given Pee Wee Marquette's money-grubbing ways, he constantly carried himself with a calm and classy demeanor. Carrying a walking stick and wearing a cummerbund, Pee Wee and Birdland seemed inseparable. His fingers would be covered with diamond-studded rings—one was a present given to him by the famous jazz vocalist Dinah Washington.

Pee Wee could be very kind to some musicians who would come to see other acts, by letting them in for free. He took good care of his friends, although his standards for friendship were mysterious and had a commercial tinge.

While working at Birdland, Pee Wee lived at the Theresa Hotel in Harlem. The bassist for Birdland, Curly Russell, lived there also and had a room next to Pee Wee. One night Curly heard some banging on the wall coming from Pee Wee's room, so he put his ear to the wall and heard Pee Wee say, "Put me down bitch, I'm gonna pay ya!"

On crowded weekend nights, you would regularly see Pee Wee searching on the floor under the Bullpen standees, wielding a lit flashlight and searching for loose change on the floor. He was usually polite about it, and customers didn't really seem to mind.

Sometimes just before dawn, with the blinding, naked cleaning lights spotlighting the ultimate horror in interior decorating—which was Birdland—he would sit on the bandstand, with microphone gripped in one sparkling little hand, singing, "South of the Border—Down Mexico Way."

COUNT BASIE ORCHESTRA

The new Basie sound of the early 1950s, with its contemporary charts and sixteen musicians, motivated Morris Levy to hire the Count Basie Orchestra to work at Birdland. It started with two weeks and soon lasted for more than a month, with Basie routinely being the band of choice during the Christmas season to New Year's Eve. Guitarist Freddie Green explains, "We would go in there and play for four to six weeks. The band sounded great at Birdland. That place was it! We would work the Waldorf in New York for a few weeks, go out of town, then come right back to Birdland. This routine went on into the early 1960s." The Basie band members looked at the gig as an opportunity to stay close to home, since most of the band were New Yorkers and enjoyed the stable income.

Count Basie backstage at Birdland in 1952.

By 1955, the African American press was running regular notices of how the band was thriving at Birdland, consistently drawing sellout crowds during its regular engagements. The *Pittsburgh Courier* reported, "Not since he came on the scene several swingcades ago has the mighty maestro met with so much approval." The paper followed up after the engagement, noting that Basie's band set a house attendance record during its two-week stay. The Basie band became so closely associated with Birdland that each new engagement was announced with a simple placard—"Basie's Back!"

During his stay at Birdland, Basie signed a record deal with Roulette Records—a company owned by Birdland proprietor Morris Levy—therefore ending his longtime relationship with Verve Records. Many questioned Basie's decision, but it was common knowledge that the Count was a compulsive gambler. He would borrow money from Levy and end up working many weeks a year at Birdland for peanuts.

Levy was central in reviving Basie's band after he had to disband his group in the early 1950s, by guaranteeing Basie regular work at Birdland and therefore laying the groundwork for the resurrection of the band. Levy's partner Morris Primack recalls, "Basie only had a six-piece band when we first booked him, so Morris Levy made him an offer. He could get his big band back together, but he must play Birdland during Easter, the 4th of July, and Christmas, or any other time he's out of work."

Basie's first appearance at Birdland with his new big band came in the summer of 1952. Basie was appreciative of the exposure Birdland would give him, as well as the chance to work with his new band. Basie states, "It's always good for a new band to have a chance to settle down somewhere and play in one place night after night for a while. Also, you couldn't wish for a better spot than Birdland. You were back in the Apple, and right on Broadway and 52nd Street, where everything was happening. You can't beat that kind of exposure. And the people running Birdland, from Morris Levy himself right down to the washroom attendants, were all for us."

With the Count Basie Orchestra blowing the roof off Birdland, business was very good, and the write-ups in the newspapers were very favorable. The constant exposure and assurance of regular income kept the band's personnel relatively stable and allowed Basie to develop a new approach that would ensure that his band remained popular for decades to come.

JOHN COLTRANE

The legendary live recording of *Live at Birdland* took place on two different nights at Birdland in 1963. A few months prior to that evening, the John Coltrane Quartet was booked at Birdland for a two-week run from July 18 to the end of the month. They were playing opposite the Terry Gibbs Quartet, featuring an attractive young pianist by the name of Alice McLeod. That evening at Birdland, she would meet John "Trane" Coltrane for the very first time, capturing not merely his eye and ear but his heart as well, and in the near future become his wife, Alice Coltrane.

Elvin Jones was Trane's main drummer during most of his Birdland gigs, except for a few times when Roy Haynes had to fill in. One particular time, Elvin was returning from the hospital, and Haynes was playing the drums with Coltrane. After the set, Roy jokingly threw the drumsticks at Elvin and said, "Go on—play with your band!"

On Tuesday, October 8, 1963, the legendary live recording by Impulse that would produce the album *Live at Birdland* would take place at Birdland. Drummer Marty Morell and saxophonist Steve Marcus were there in the audience that evening to witness history in the making. The group would also record later that month on October 18th for additional album tracks.

On July 30, 1964, there was a chance to have a historic meeting of two giants, Miles Davis and John Coltrane, playing at Birdland on the very same evening, but Miles unfortunately canceled. Miles was famous for his last-minute cancellations. They had worked together at Birdland in the early 1950s, but only as sidemen.

On January 12, 1965, the John Coltrane Quartet signed a monthlong contract with Birdland, opposite the Mose Allison Trio and the Bud Powell Trio. The *New Yorker* magazine ran a series of articles that month and the next, stating, "The foursome of John Coltrane, whose saxophone is both puissant [a later article used the word "penetrating"] and long in the wind, is spelled by the threesome of Mose Allison . . . ," and "What happens here [at Birdland] is frequently a well-kept secret; nevertheless, a rumor has it that a trio run by Bud Powell, that truly mystic pianist, and a foursome run by John Coltrane, who hates to tear himself from his saxophone for more than a minute, are in residence. But subject-to-change-without-notice is often the way of life here [at Birdland]. At any rate, whoever is on deck now will be replaced on Thursday, Feb. 11." Sadly, Birdland would never need a replacement. They would close the doors for good on the Jazz Corner of the World, never to reopen but for one night in November 1977.

John Coltrane Quartet at Birdland in the early 1960s with McCoy Tyner, Jimmy Garrison, and Elvin Jones. Anthony and Mary Boulanger are tabled up front.

ART BLAKEY QUINTET

The Art Blakey Quintet's performance on the live recording *A Night at Birdland* was captured by Blue Note's Alfred Lion and recording engineer Rudy Van Gelder at Birdland on February 21, 1954. The complete evening of five sets, which included Clifford Brown on trumpet, Lou Donaldson on alto sax, Horace Silver on piano, Curly Russell on bass, and Art Blakey on drums, went off without a hitch. Although this live recording was released as the Art Blakey Quintet, the record was not supposed to be a Blakey-led session, but rather a session known as the "Blue Note All-Stars."

On the night of the recording, Blakey tracked down Birdland's emcee, Pee Wee Marquette, and gave him a few dollars to announce the band as the Art Blakey All-Stars instead of the Blue Note All-Stars.

When the time came, Pee Wee stepped up to the microphone and announced, "So we're bringing back to the bandstand the great Art Blakey and his wonderful group, featuring the new trumpet sensation Clifford Brown, Horace Silver on piano, Lou Donaldson on alto, Curly Russell is on bass. Let's get together and bring Art Blakey to the bandstand with a great big round of applause. How about a big hand there? Art Blakey—hey ya'll!" Soon after the introduction, Horace Silver looks to Lou Donaldson and says, "What the heck is happening?" And Lou says, "I don't know, and I'm not going to ask."

A few days before the recording, Art Blakey and the band would rehearse at Birdland during the afternoon hours, when the club was closed. During one of the rehearsals, Miles Davis walks in and sits down for a while, and he proceeds to listen to the band's rehearsal. Before he was about to leave, he looked up at Clifford Brown and said jokingly, "Clifford, I hope you bust your chops," and then he laughed and left. The bassist Curly Russell said to Clifford, "He wasn't joking when he said that. He really meant it."

This recording made jazz history by being the first of its kind ever to be recorded at a live venue, using a major record label's equipment. *A Night at Birdland* showcased the birth of hard bop and set up the framework for Art Blakey's next musical adventure—the Jazz Messengers.

Blakey always gave one hundred percent of himself and expected the band to do the same. Art would tell the band at Birdland, "I don't care what kind of problems you got with your wife, or at home. When you come in here, be prepared to cook. Leave your problems outside."

OPPOSITE The Art Blakey Quintet at Birdland in February 1954; Clifford Brown (trumpet), Horace Silver (piano), Curly Russell (bass), Lou Donaldson (alto sax), and Art Blakey (drums).

CHAPTER THREE

MARCEL FLEISS

BIRDLAND PHOTOS

Marcel Fleiss arrived in New York City from Paris, France, in the early 1950s and at the age of seventeen was allowed entrance to Birdland by the manager, Oscar Goodstein, who gave him special permission to watch and photograph the jazz musicians as long as he consumed only soft drinks.

During his many visits to Birdland, Marcel Fleiss captured many iconic images and developed a close friendship with many of the jazz musicians, including a lifelong friendship with Goodstein.

Since his return to Paris in 1954, Marcel would receive letters from many of the jazz musicians he befriended while spending time at Birdland and in New York City. He received letters from John Lewis, J. J. Johnson, Charles Mingus, and Gigi Gryce, who would mention that Clifford Brown sends his regards and that his French is improving.

Marcel Fleiss was known not only for his iconic photographs, but also for the jazz column he wrote in the Jazz Hot magazine—the oldest and most respected publication in France and throughout Europe. He would also display his many jazz photographs in the magazine. Marcel wrote the first article and biography about Charles Mingus in *Jazz Hot*.

Today, Marcel Fleiss is the founder and owner of the Galerie 1900–2000 in Paris, France.

LEFT TO RIGHT Marcel Fleiss with jazz piano greats Art Tatum, Erroll Garner, and Count Basie in the early 1950s. *©Marcel Fleiss/CTSIMAGES*

ABOVE Miles Davis, Roy Haynes, and Charlie Parker at Birdland in 1951. ©*Marcel Fleiss/CTSIMAGES*

OPPOSITE TOP Charlie Parker and strings at Birdland in 1951. ©*Marcel Fleiss/CTSIMAGES*

OPPOSITE BELOW George Shearing Quintet at Birdland in 1952. Left to right:
George Shearing (piano), Don Elliott (vibes), Al McKibbon (bass), Denzil Best (drums),
and Chuck Wayne (guitar). ©*Marcel Fleiss/CTSIMAGES*

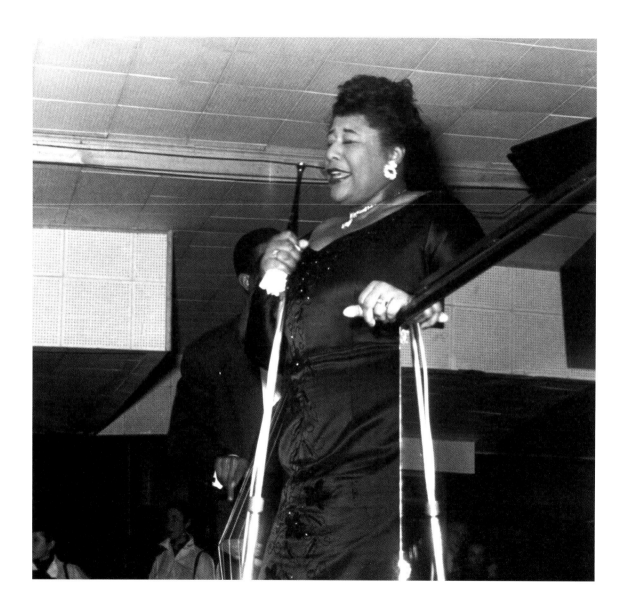

Ella Fitzgerald at Birdland in the early 1950s. *©Marcel Fleiss/CTSIMAGES*

Red Rodney and Zoot Sims at Birdland in 1951. *©Marcel Fleiss/CTSIMAGES*

OPPOSITE Billie Holiday (center) with Sarah Vaughan (left) and Slim Gaillard at Birdland in 1952. *©Marcel Fleiss/CTSIMAGES*

ABOVE Stan Getz Quintet at Birdland in 1952; Stan Getz (tenor sax), Duke Jordan (piano), Jimmy Raney (guitar), Charles Mingus (bass), and Phil Brown (drums). *©Marcel Fleiss/CTSIMAGES*

Jazz piano greats Erroll Garner and Art Tatum at Birdland in the early 1950s.
©Marcel Fleiss/CTSIMAGES

Trumpeters Roy Eldridge and Miles Davis in the sound booth at Birdland with DJ "Symphony Sid" Torin on April 13, 1951. *©Marcel Fleiss/CTSIMAGES*

ABOVE Art Blakey at Birdland in the early 1950s. *©Marcel Fleiss/CTSIMAGES*

OPPOSITE TOP Lester Young with vocalist Joe Carroll and bassist Gene Ramey at Birdland in 1951. *©Marcel Fleiss/CTSIMAGES*

OPPOSITE BELOW Max Roach and Zoot Sims at Birdland (Christmas 1952). *©Marcel Fleiss/CTSIMAGES*

One of many letters sent to Marcel Fleiss from his good friend and manager of Birdland, Oscar Goodstein.

CHAPTER FOUR

BIOGRAPHIES

OF SELECT BIRDLAND MUSICIANS

Julian "Cannonball" Adderley (1928–1975). Tampa, Florida. Helped define the hard bop sound with his combination of flawless technique on the alto saxophone, and his effortless ability to meld the blues, gospel, and funk. He would usually work with his brother Nat Adderley on trumpet/cornet.

Mose Allison (1927–2016). Tippo, Mississippi. A jazz and blues pianist, singer, and songwriter, known for playing a unique mix of blues and modern jazz, both singing and playing piano.

Gene "Jug" Ammons (1925–1974). Chicago, Illinois. Known as "the Boss," Ammons was a pioneering tenor saxophonist with a huge, soulful tone, and the innate ability to make a tune his own, contributing to a musical styling known as "Soul Jazz."

Pearl Bailey (1918–1990). Newport News, Virginia. A notable actress and sultry singer that started out with Count Basie and Cab Calloway, later acting on Broadway and in such films as Porgy and Bess, and receiving the Presidential Medal of Freedom in 1988.

Chet Baker (1929–1988). Yale, Oklahoma. Jazz trumpeter/singer and exponent of the West Coast school of cool jazz, Baker had an intimate and captivating playing and singing style. Although battling drug addiction for most of his life, Chet continued to produce masterful performances.

Louie Bellson (1924–2009). Rock Falls, Illinois. Drummer, composer, jazz educator, and bandleader, Bellson was a superlative drummer who worked with most of the big bands during the 1940s and 1950s. Duke Ellington called him "the world's greatest drummer." A prolific composer, Bellson wrote more than 1,000 compositions and arrangements during his lifetime.

George Benson (1943–). Pittsburgh, Pennsylvania. Guitarist and singer-songwriter with terrific speed and tone, and could play many musical styles. Although one of the greatest guitarists in jazz history, Benson had a singing style and tone that was lush and soulful.

Bob Brookmeyer (1929–2011). Kansas City, Missouri. First gained attention as a member of Gerry Mulligan's quartet. A top valve trombonist and pianist, and highly revered composer/arranger, Bob in later years would lead the Thad Jones / Mel Lewis Orchestra, and notably his own "New Art Orchestra."

Clifford Brown (1930–1956). Wilmington, Delaware. Jazz trumpeter with power, range, and brilliance, together with warmth and invention. His first live jazz album, *A Night at Birdland*, with the Art Blakey Quintet, is a jazz classic. Sadly, Clifford died at the age of twenty-five in a car accident.

Dave Brubeck (1920–2012). Concord, California. A pianist known for compositions with unusual time signatures and meters and for superimposing contrasting rhythms. His legendary quartet would include alto saxophonist Paul Desmond, who played on Brubeck's jazz classic, "Take Five."

Ron Carter (1937–). Ferndale, Michigan. With over 2,000 recording sessions to his credit, Carter is certainly the most recorded jazz bassist in history. A rhythmic and melodic player with a full, fat sound. He is undeniably one of the greatest accompanists of all time.

Arnett Cobb (1918–1989). Houston, Texas. Originator of the "Southern Preacher" style of playing, with that bar-walking tenor saxophone sound that earned him the nickname "Wild Man of the Tenor Sax." Cobb would captivate audiences worldwide with his uninhibited playing style.

Eddie "Lockjaw" Davis (1922–1986). Columbus, Ohio. "Jaws" had one of the most unmistakable tenor saxophone sounds—full bodied, gutsy, and hard driving, with a warmth and depth for playing slow, tender ballads. Known for his starring role with the Count Basie Band, especially when featured on "Jumpin' at the Woodside" and "Whirlybird."

Miles Davis (1926–1991). Alton, Illinois. One of the most recognized and influential jazz artists in the history of jazz, having been involved with almost every important innovation and stylistic development. Miles's trumpet sound was instantly recognizable—cool, ethereal, and romantic, with an innate feel for space, silence, and tonality. Many of his original compositions became classics, such as "All Blues," "Nardis," and "Milestones."

Sammy Davis Jr. (1925–1990). New York City. With the nickname "Mr. Show Business," Sammy started his career in vaudeville with his father at the age of three and was known in later life as someone who could do it all—sing, dance, do stand-up, and play many musical instruments. He will forever be remembered as a member of the legendary "Rat Pack" in Las Vegas.

Buddy DeFranco (1923–2014). Camden, New Jersey. One of a few clarinetists who played bebop, he was often dubbed "the Charlie Parker of the clarinet." Buddy had a smooth, precise, and lyrical approach to playing, and a ceaseless energy for experimentation.

Paul Desmond (1924–1977). San Francisco, California. Spent most of his professional career playing alto saxophone with the Dave Brubeck Quartet, and was noted for composing the famous jazz standard "Take Five." Paul was known for his light, sweet, and melodic tone on the alto.

Eric Dolphy (1928–1964). Los Angeles, California. A groundbreaking jazz alto saxophonist, bass clarinetist, and flutist known for his avant-garde, free-jazz style of playing. His soloing style utilized the 12-tone scale, in addition to the use of false fingerings to create a multiphonic effect on his saxophone.

Kenny Dorham (1924–1972). Fairfax, Texas. Jazz trumpeter with an identifiable soft, soothing sound. His lyrical improvisations and articulated swing feel, along with his mastery and gifted approach to ballad playing, made him first call for many all-star groups.

Billy Eckstine (1914–1993). Pittsburgh, Pennsylvania. Legendary singer of ballads and bandleader of the swing era, known for his smooth baritone voice and distinctive vibrato. The Billy Eckstine Orchestra was the first bop big band of its time, employing many up-and-coming jazz artists.

Harry "Sweets" Edison (1915–1999). Columbus, Ohio. A bandleader and band member of the Count Basie Orchestra, and one of the hardest-swinging, bluesiest jazz trumpeters of the twentieth century. Edison played at Birdland many times during the late 1950s.

Roy Eldridge (1911–1989). Pittsburgh, Pennsylvania. Nicknamed "Little Jazz," Eldridge was an exciting trumpeter with a competitive spirit and chance-taking soloing style. Roy played at Birdland in 1951 with his own all-star band for Symphony Sid's "A Battle of Jazz Trumpets."

Duke Ellington (1899–1974). Washington, DC. Pianist, composer, originator of big-band jazz, and leader of the Duke Ellington Orchestra from 1923 until his passing in 1974. Duke composed thousands of scores over his fifty-year career, including the swing hits "Satin Doll" and "It Don't Mean a Thing If It Ain't Got That Swing."

Bill Evans (1929–1980). Plainfield, New Jersey. Jazz composer and pianist who primarily worked in a trio setting. Evans's use of block chords, interpretation of jazz standards, and hard-swinging melodic lines are legendary. Bill Evans played Birdland many times over the years, including the memorable live recordings in 1960, with Scott LaFaro on bass and Paul Motian on drums.

Art Farmer (1928–1999). Council Bluffs, Iowa. A highly melodic soloist known for his individuality, lyricism, warmth of tone, and sensitivity both on trumpet and flügelhorn. Farmer recorded more than fifty albums under his name, and dozens more with other leaders.

Maynard Ferguson (1928–2006). Verdun, Quebec. Canadian jazz trumpeter and bandleader known for his piercing power and screaming high notes. Maynard came to prominence playing lead with Stan Kenton and later formed his own band. Ferguson played at Birdland in 1956–57 with his fourteen-piece big band, recording, in the studio, *Maynard Ferguson and His Birdland Dream Band*.

Ella Fitzgerald (1917–1996). Newport News, Virginia. Known as the "First Lady of Song," Ella's beautiful voice and wide range could outswing anyone. A brilliant scat singer who always sounded and looked happy to be singing. During her lengthy career, Ella won thirteen Grammys and sold over forty million records.

Slim Gaillard (1916–1991). Detroit, Michigan. Jazz singer and multi-instrumentalist who was noted for his comedic "vocalese" singing—scat singing using improvised nonsense syllables, such as "bee bop da bwee dee." Gaillard frequently opened at Birdland for acts such as Charlie Parker, Dizzy Gillespie, and Billie Holiday, to name a few.

Erroll Garner (1923–1977). Pittsburgh, Pennsylvania. Brilliant jazz pianist and composer with one of the most distinctive sounds of all time. Garner played with such enthusiasm, having the ability to play stunning runs while displaying pure joy. His ballad composition "Misty" has become a jazz standard.

Stan Getz (1927–1991). Philadelphia, Pennsylvania. Tenor saxophonist and composer with exceptional talent and sound—known for his warm, wispy, lyrical tone and virtuosic playing—was considered one of the greatest tenor saxophonists of all time. Getz was perhaps best known for popularizing bossa nova music with the hit "The Girl from Ipanema."

Benny Golson (1929–). Philadelphia, Pennsylvania. Tenor saxophonist and talented composer/arranger who wrote such jazz standards as "I Remember Clifford," "Killer Joe," and "Whisper Not." Golson was best known for his stint with Art Blakey's Jazz Messengers, and his virtuosic command of the tenor saxophone.

Dexter Gordon (1923–1990). Los Angeles, California. Sometimes referred to as "Long Tall Dexter," Gordon was one of the earliest tenor saxophonists to play bebop. His huge sound, melodic playing style, laid-back feel, and innate ability to communicate with audiences were legendary.

Johnny Griffin (1928–2008). Chicago, Illinois. One of the all-time-great tenor saxophonists, remembered as a player of tender ballads and a performer who could effortlessly negotiate difficult chord changes at breakneck tempos. A highly revered master of the tenor saxophone.

Friedrich Gulda (1930–2000). Vienna, Austria. Pianist and composer known for his classical playing as a child prodigy in the mid-1940s, Gulda delved into jazz in his early adulthood after hearing Count Basie, which led to recording a live album at Birdland on June 28, 1956.

Lionel Hampton (1908–2002). Louisville, Kentucky. Bandleader, drummer, and the first jazz vibraphonist. Lionel worked with Armstrong and Goodman before forming his own big band in 1940, rising to prominence with such hits as "Flying Home," "Hamp's Boogie Woogie," and "Hey! Ba-Ba-Re-Bop."

Slide Hampton (1932–). Jeannette, Pennsylvania. Described by the critics as a master composer, arranger, and gifted trombonist, Hampton helped keep bop alive both in his writing and playing. In later life he became a renowned clinician, and a role model for a new generation of trombonists.

Herbie Hancock (1940–). Chicago, Illinois. Pianist, keyboardist, bandleader, and composer, Hancock was one of the primary architects of the post-bop sound, and one of the first jazz musicians to utilize synthesizers in his music. Hancock's sound is entirely his own—able to absorb funk, gospel, and blues.

Coleman Hawkins (1904–1969). Saint Joseph, Missouri. Pioneer of the tenor saxophone and influence to many up-and-coming jazz musicians, he was always at the top of his game over his long career within the changing music scenes. Hawkins will forever be remembered for his stellar performance on the ballad "Body and Soul."

Roy Haynes (1925–). Boston, Massachusetts. With a career spanning more than seventy years, Haynes worked with Lester Young and Bud Powell and was a member of Charlie Parker's quintet from 1949 to 1952, performing on many live Birdland recordings and radio broadcasts.

Joe Henderson (1937–2001). Lima, Ohio. Jazz tenor saxophonist and composer, becoming a dominant force early in his career, revered for his distinctive sound and powers of invention. His playing encompassed bebop, hard-bop, and rhythm and blues, as well as Latin and avant-garde.

Woody Herman (1913–1987). Milwaukee, Wisconsin. Starting off in vaudeville as "the Boy Wonder of the Clarinet," Herman led the most varied and successful big band, the so-called Thundering Herd, in the history of jazz. His famous showstoppers were "Woodchopper's Ball," "Four Brothers," and "Caldonia."

Billie Holiday (1915–1959). Philadelphia, Pennsylvania. One of the greatest and most influential singers in the history of jazz. Her poignant renditions of songs and incredible depth of emotion added a new dimension to jazz singing. Although Billie lived a difficult life plagued by alcohol and drug abuse, she left behind a body of work that continues to inspire singers and listeners alike.

Freddie Hubbard (1938–2008). Indianapolis, Indiana. An inspirational and dynamic soloist both on trumpet and flügelhorn, Hubbard had an unmistakable and influential sound. Forming his sound out of Clifford Brown / Lee Morgan, he continued to be a pacesetter through the 1960s and 1970s, releasing such fine albums as *Red Clay* and *Straight Life*.

Bobby Hutcherson (1941–2016). Los Angeles, California. One of the greatest jazz vibraphonists, Bobby helped redefine the capabilities of the instrument, both technically and emotionally. An artist comfortable both in post-bop and experimental free jazz, Hutcherson's work remains entirely compelling.

Illinois Jacquet (1922–2004). Broussard, Louisiana. An influential tenor saxophonist and bandleader who gained popularity by playing a wailing solo on Lionel Hampton's 1942 recording "Flying Home." A masterful, dynamic soloist, Jacquet would lead his big band until his death at eighty-one years old.

J. J. Johnson (1924–2001). Indianapolis, Indiana. One of the finest jazz trombonists of all time, Johnson played with such ease and speed that listeners thought he was playing a valve trombone. Virtuosity aside, Johnson played with such feeling, passion, and soul, coupled with his rich, dark tone.

Elvin Jones (1927–2004). Pontiac, Michigan. Considered the most influential drummer in the history of jazz, Elvin transformed the drums from being only a time-keeping instrument to an instrument that created a dynamic interplay with soloists. Jones's joining Coltrane in 1960 was historic—recording the legendary *Live at Birdland* album in 1964.

Hank Jones (1918–2010). Vicksburg, Mississippi. Pianist, arranger/composer, and bandleader who was described as eloquent, lyrical, and impeccable. Jones would accompany Ella Fitzgerald from 1948 to 1953 and make several musically historic recordings with Charlie Parker. He was a pianist with exceptional taste and sophistication.

Philly Joe Jones (1923–1985). Philadelphia, Pennsylvania. Came to fame with the Miles Davis Quintet; a masterful accompanist and dynamic drummer who worked with the greatest names in jazz, such as Charlie Parker, Dizzy Gillespie, and Lionel Hampton, to name a few.

Quincy Jones (1933–). Chicago, Illinois. Known affectionately as "Q," Quincy is an arranger/composer, musician, and producer. His career has spanned over seven decades. A distinguished bandleader, sideman, solo artist, record label executive, movie producer, and a book author. Jones has worked with the best in the music business, from Frank Sinatra to Michael Jackson.

Thad Jones (1923–1986). Pontiac, Michigan. Arranger/composer, bandleader, and trumpeter/cornetist, Thad started out with Count Basie as a trumpet soloist, later leaving to become a freelance arranger and musician in New York City. Only two years later he would form, along with Mel Lewis, the legendary Thad Jones / Mel Lewis Orchestra.

Stan Kenton (1911–1979). Wichita, Kansas. Pianist, composer/arranger, and bandleader who led an influential and innovative big band. Kenton's sound was controversial, with advanced harmonies, progressive rhythms, and tonalities. The Stan Kenton Orchestra would play at Birdland many times during the 1950s.

Rahsaan Roland Kirk (1935–1977). Columbus, Ohio. Tenor saxophonist, flutist, and multi-instrumentalist, Kirk was a postmodernist, and one of the most exciting soloists in jazz history. Onstage he would play up to three horns at once, including flutes and whistles; this setup would allow him to function as a one-man saxophone section.

Lee Konitz (1927–). Chicago, Illinois. Alto saxophonist with a distinctive and individual style, known for playing bebop, cool jazz, and avant-garde. Konitz would become associated with the cool-jazz movement—playing on Miles Davis's *Birth of the Cool* album. He would also play with Lennie Tristano at the official opening of Birdland on December 15, 1949.

Michel Legrand (1932–). Courbevoie, France. Pianist, composer/arranger, conductor, and a master composer of countless musical compositions and movie soundtracks, who has collaborated with a wide range of musical artists—from Miles Davis to Barbra Streisand.

Ramsey Lewis (1935–). Chicago, Illinois. Pianist and composer, Ramsey has been a contemporary-jazz figure since the late 1950s, playing music with a warm, personal flare, which has allowed him to cross over to pop and R & B, recording over eighty albums, receiving seven gold records, and accepting three Grammy Awards.

Machito (1908–1984). Havana, Cuba. Latin jazz singer who helped redefine Afro-Cuban jazz and create Cubop and salsa music. Machito formed the band Afro-Cubans in New York City in 1940 and would go on to play at Birdland throughout the 1950s, inspiring many jazz artists with his Latin rhythms.

Jackie McLean (1931–2006). New York City. Alto saxophonist, composer, bandleader, and educator who performed with jazz greats Charlie Parker and Miles Davis. Jackie was one of the few bop-oriented players to play free jazz in the 1960s, later teaching and mentoring a new generation of jazz artists as an educator.

Marian McPartland (1918–2013). Slough, Berkshire, England. Pianist, composer, and radio host who played such jazz stylings as bebop, cool jazz, swing, and post-bop and is known for her harmonic and rhythmic complexity and extensive knowledge of jazz standards. Her involvement in over sixty years of jazz has been well documented.

Carmen McRae (1922–1994). Harlem, New York. Singer known for her unique singing style with behind-the-beat phrasing and wry interpretation of lyrics. She would sing with big bands such as Count Basie, Benny Carter, and Mercer Ellington, leading her own trio and recording up to 1989.

Charles Mingus (1922–1979). Nogales, Arizona. Bassist, pianist, composer, and bandleader, Mingus favored complex rhythms, dissonant harmonies, and free improvisation. Early on he worked as a sideman with Armstrong and Hampton, later performing and recording with Charlie Parker, Bud Powell, and Miles Davis at Birdland.

Blue Mitchell (1930–1979). Miami, Florida. Trumpeter best known as a lyrical and hard-swinging player, with innate talent and a clear tone. Mitchell first became noticed as a member of Horace Silver's quintet, where he polished his hard-bop skills. He was one of the most melodic players of his generation.

Hank Mobley (1930–1986). Eastman, Georgia. Tenor saxophonist and founding member of the original Jazz Messengers, Mobley gained experience in the bands of Dizzy Gillespie and Max Roach and helped form the hard-bop movement. Mobley's playing was sweet and precise, with solo lines full of intricate rhythmic patterns.

Modern Jazz Quartet (1952–1993). Jazz combo that performed for over forty years, playing cool jazz, bebop, blues, and classical music. The group consisted of John Lewis (piano), Milt Jackson (vibraphone), Percy Heath (bass), and Connie Kay (drums). Their repertoire included bop and swing pieces, and originals such as "Django" and "Bags Groove."

Thelonious Monk (1917–1982). Rocky Mount, North Carolina. Pianist, composer, and one of the first creators of modern jazz, Monk had a playful improvisational style that featured dissonances, with a percussive piano approach. Many of his compositions have become jazz standards, including "Well, You Needn't," "Blue Monk," and "Round Midnight."

Lee Morgan (1938–1972). Philadelphia, Pennsylvania. One of hard bop's greatest trumpeters, a master of his instrument who modeled himself after Clifford Brown. Morgan had a virtuosic technique, powerful in the high register and sweet and sensitive on ballads. Had great success with his boogaloo-style original composition "Sidewinder."

Gerry Mulligan (1927–1996). Queens, New York. Known as one of the most widely respected and admired jazz musicians of our time, and the leading baritone saxophonist in jazz history, Mulligan was also a talented composer and arranger, as well as a skilled pianist. His compositions and arrangements were an invaluable contribution to the landmark recording *Birth of the Cool*.

Fats Navarro (1923–1950). Key West, Florida. Jazz trumpet virtuoso and one of the founders of bebop, Navarro was a leading trumpeter in the 1940s, working with Tad Dameron, Bud Powell, and Charles Mingus. He played beautiful melodies with a fat, sweet tone. His final performance was with Charlie Parker at Birdland in 1950.

Phineas Newborn Jr. (1931–1989). Whiteville, Tennessee. One of the most technically skilled and brilliant pianists in jazz, able to perform brisk, complex solos with both hands in unison. In his prime, Phineas was nothing short of a jazz piano phenomenon—right up there with Bud Powell and Art Tatum.

Chico O'Farrill (1921–2001). Havana, Cuba. Composer, arranger, conductor, and bandleader, Chico wrote arrangements for Benny Goodman and Stan Kenton and contributed to several Afro-Cuban jazz works by Charlie Parker and Dizzy Gillespie. His band, the Afro-Cuban Jazz Orchestra, recorded and played at Birdland many times over the years.

Oscar Peterson (1925–2007). Montreal, Quebec. Considered one of the greatest jazz pianists, Peterson released over 200 recordings and won eight Grammys and numerous other awards and honors, including the revered Order of Canada. A pianist with technique on the level of Art Tatum, Oscar's speed, precision, and the ability to swing at any tempo are legendary.

Bud Powell (1924–1966). Harlem, New York. A giant of the jazz piano, and the most important pianist in the bebop style, Powell was influenced at an early age by Art Tatum and was later tutored by Thelonious Monk. Bud's immeasurable contribution and influence on other musicians was astounding. A musical genius—powerful, engaging, and giving.

Tito Puente (1923–2000). New York City. "King of Latin Jazz" or "El Rey" was a percussionist, composer, and record producer. Puente was a pioneer, known for mixing musical styles with Latin sounds, and the infusion of Latin music with jazz. A highly revered musician and musical legend in Latin music and jazz, recording over 200 albums.

Buddy Rich (1917–1987). Brooklyn, New York. Considered one of the best jazz drummers and big-band leaders in the history of jazz, Buddy was recognized for his virtuoso technique, speed, power, and precision. Buddy was sometimes known for his short temper, and his impressive career spanned over sixty years—from working as a child star in vaudeville to leading his own world famous big band for decades.

Max Roach (1924–2007). Newland, North Carolina. Drummer, percussionist, composer, and a pioneer of bebop, Roach is considered one of the most important and influential jazz drummers in history. Having worked with the who's who of the jazz world, Max was awarded many musical achievement awards and honorary doctorate degrees.

Red Rodney (1927–1994). Philadelphia, Pennsylvania. Born Robert Chudnick, he became best known for his association with Charlie Parker—joining the Charlie Parker Quintet in 1949. A creative and inspirational bebop jazz trumpeter, who after playing with Parker would lead his own quintet, playing with Ira Sullivan and later with saxophonist Chris Potter.

Tito Rodriguez (1923–1973). Santurce, Puerto Rico. Singer, percussionist, and bandleader known by many as "El Involvidable." Tito was a talented vocalist with his own distinctive singing style. He would record and play at Birdland with his band the Tito Rodriguez Orchestra.

Sonny Rollins (1930–). New York City. One of the most recognized and enduring tenor saxophonists in jazz. His harmonically innovative ideas and rhythmic solos continue to influence and inspire the next generation of jazz musicians. Some of his original compositions include "St. Thomas," "Oleo," and "Airegin."

George Shearing (1919–2011). London, England. Pianist with a unique quintet sound, which featured piano, vibraphone, electric guitar, bass, and drums. Shearing composed over 300 musical compositions, which included the jazz standard "Lullaby of Birdland," composed in 1952 when he was working at Birdland.

Wayne Shorter (1933–). Newark, New Jersey. Saxophonist and composer who played with Horace Silver and Art Blakey's Jazz Messengers in the 1950s, later joining the Miles Davis Quintet in the 1960s and cofounding the band Weather Report in 1970. An intriguing saxophonist and prolific composer of such tunes as "Nefertiti," "Footprints," and "ESP."

Horace Silver (1928–2014). New Rochelle, New York. Jazz pianist and composer who cofounded the legendary Jazz Messengers and pioneered the jazz style called hard bop. Silver influenced generations of musicians with original compositions such as "Nica's Dream" and "Song for My Father." He worked often at Birdland throughout the 1950s.

Zoot Sims (1925–1985). Inglewood, California. Tenor saxophonist who gained attention in the "Four Brothers" sax section of Woody Herman, later launching a long, successful solo career, partnering at times with Al Cohn or Bob Brookmeyer. Sims's natural sense of swing, distinctive sound, and melodic creativity are legendary.

Sonny Stitt (1924–1982). Boston, Massachusetts. Tenor and alto saxophonist who has made more recordings as a bandleader than any other jazz instrumentalist. Sonny was equipped with incredible technique and an innate ability to swing, often teaming up with fellow tenor player Gene Ammons for their legendary tenor battles.

Art Tatum (1909–1956). Toledo, Ohio. One of the greatest and most influential jazz pianists of all time. Tatum's virtuosic technique set the new standard for all jazz pianists. His speed, precision, and creative imagination kept him in a league of his own. Art's performances of "Tiger Rag" and "Tea for Two" showcase his mastery of stride piano.

Clark Terry (1920–2015). St. Louis, Missouri. Swing and bebop trumpeter, and pioneer of the flügelhorn in jazz, Terry developed one of the most distinctive sounds in jazz history. One of his showstoppers utilized his unique scat-singing ability, which led to his notable hit "Mumbles."

Bobby Timmons (1935–1974). Philadelphia, Pennsylvania. Pianist and composer, and sideman in Art Blakey's Jazz Messengers and Cannonball Adderley's band. A bebop pianist who could play and compose infectious, funky tunes such as "Moanin'" and "Dat Dere," which helped generate the soul jazz style.

Toshiko Mariano Quartet Japanese jazz pianist Toshiko Akiyoshi married jazz alto saxophonist Charlie Mariano in the early 1960s, therefore becoming Toshiko Mariano. The Toshiko Mariano Quartet played and recorded the album *Live at Birdland* at the legendary club in 1960–61.

Lennie Tristano (1919–1978). Chicago, Illinois. Pianist, composer, arranger, and educator, moved to New York City in the late 1940s and performed with Charlie Parker and Dizzy Gillespie. His complex harmonic and rhythmic approach to jazz improvisation was ahead of its time and was often misunderstood by critics and listeners alike. Tristano played at the opening of Birdland in 1949 and worked there often during the 1950s.

McCoy Tyner (1938–). Philadelphia, Pennsylvania. Pianist and composer who rose to notoriety working with the John Coltrane Quartet in the 1960s. Tyner's piano style can be distinguished by his strong left-handed bass and right-handed fourth-interval chord voicings. He is considered to be one of the most influential jazz pianists of the twentieth century.

Sarah Vaughan (1924–1990). Newark, New Jersey. Jazz singer with a four-octave vocal range, from soprano to baritone, and a variety of vocal textures; had an innate ability to scat sing like an instrument solo. "The Divine One" or "Sassy," as she was affectionately named, starred and recorded live at Birdland on many occasions.

Dinah Washington (1924–1963). Tuscaloosa, Alabama. Jazz singer with the title of "Queen of the Blues" was one of the most popular vocalists and recording artists of the 1950s. Her gritty, high-pitched voice, clarity of diction, and bluesy phrasing packed clubs and concert halls from New York to Vegas.

Ben Webster (1909–1973). Kansas City, Missouri. Considered one of the three most important swing tenor saxophonists, along with Lester Young and Coleman Hawkins; was affectionately known as "the Brute." Webster's sound on tenor could be warm and tender on ballads, and large and raspy on stomps. Known for his work with Fletcher Henderson and Duke Ellington, Ben played at Birdland in the 1950s, recording a live album there in 1952.

Joe Williams (1918–1999). Cordele, Georgia. Singer with the Count Basie Orchestra from 1954 to 1961. Williams was the last great big-band singer, with a smooth, dark-timbered baritone voice that could outswing anyone. He helped revive the Basie band with hits such as "Every Day I Have the Blues," and "Alright, Okay, You Win."

Kai Winding (1922–1983). Aarhus, Denmark. Trombonist and composer well known for coleading one of the most popular jazz groups of the mid-1950s with jazz trombonist J. J. Johnson. After the team broke up, Winding formed a septet featuring four trombones and a rhythm section in 1956. Kai could be seen playing Birdland with his septet often during the late 1950s.

Phil Woods (1931–2015). Springfield, Massachusetts. Alto saxophonist, bandleader, and composer who developed into an incredible saxophonist and inspiration for future generations of musicians. A powerhouse bandleader and sideman with Monk and Quincy Jones, Woods would marry Charlie Parker's widow, Chan Parker, spending almost twenty years with her.

Lester Young (1909–1959). Woodville, Mississippi. Known as "Prez," a tenor saxophonist who came to prominence with Count Basie's orchestra, having a cool, relaxed tone with a free-floating style. Lester's playing style influenced many tenor players of the day, such as Stan Getz and Zoot Sims. Young would play at the opening of Birdland on December 15, 1949, with Stan Getz.

CHAPTER FIVE

BIRDLAND

HANDBILLS

Opening **THURSDAY NITE, DECEMBER 15, 1949, at 8 P.M.** — Limited Engagement

Merry Xmas

ADMISSION **98¢** INCLUDING TAX

For Reservations COlumbus 5-9056

BIRDLAND

BROADWAY & 52nd STREET

Happy New Year

ADMISSION **98¢** INCLUDING TAX

For Reservations COlumbus 5-9056

PRESENTS AN

ALL-AMERICAN JAZZ FESTIVAL

JOURNEY THRU JAZZ 1820-1950
FEATURING

Concerts of AMERICA'S OWN MUSIC from DIXIELAND to BOP 8 P.M. to 4 A.M. Nightly

AND STARRING

ORAN "HOT LIPS"
PAGE
MAX
KAMINSKY
and his Dixielanders
GEORGE WETTLING
MUNN WARE
DICK HYMAN
IRVING LANG
SOL YAGED

The 2 "Coolest" Tenor Men
LESTER
YOUNG
The "Prez" of Swing
and
STAN
GETZ
Winter of this Year's
METRONOME
All-Star Poll

CHARLIE
PARKER
and his Quintet
RED RODNEY
TOMMY POTTER
AL HAIG
ROY HAINES
That Great Young Vocalist
HARRY
BELAFONTE

LENNIE
TRISTANO
SEXTET
LEE KONITZ
BILLY BAUER
WARREN MARSH
ARNOLD FISHKIN
JEFF MORTON
and Introducing
FLORENCE WRIGHT
Bill Cook's Singing Find

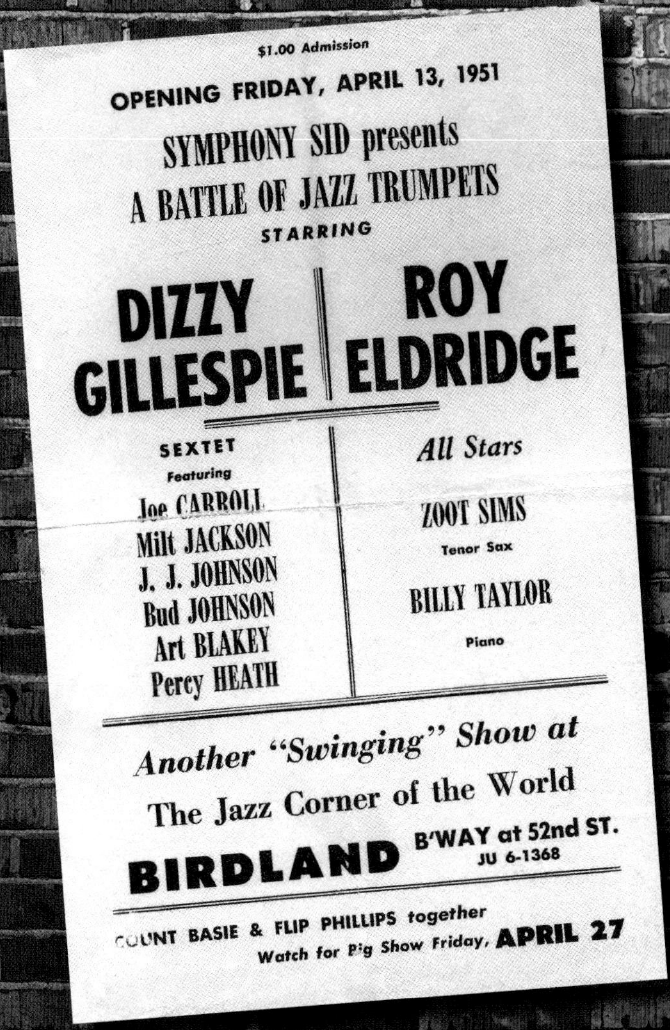

$1.00 Admission

OPENING FRIDAY, APRIL 13, 1951

SYMPHONY SID presents

A BATTLE OF JAZZ TRUMPETS

STARRING

DIZZY GILLESPIE | ROY ELDRIDGE

SEXTET	All Stars
Featuring	
Joe CARROLL	ZOOT SIMS
Milt JACKSON	Tenor Sax
J. J. JOHNSON	
Bud JOHNSON	BILLY TAYLOR
Art BLAKEY	Piano
Percy HEATH	

Another "Swinging" Show at

The Jazz Corner of the World

BIRDLAND
B'WAY at 52nd ST.
JU 6-1368

COUNT BASIE & FLIP PHILLIPS together

Watch for Big Show Friday, **APRIL 27**

1951

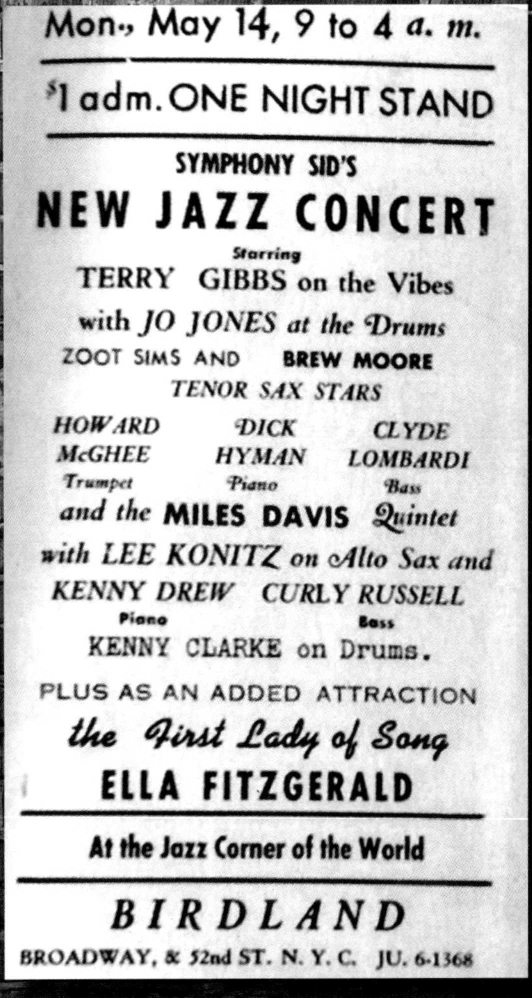

Mon., May 14, 9 to 4 a. m.

$1 adm. ONE NIGHT STAND

SYMPHONY SID'S

NEW JAZZ CONCERT

Starring

TERRY GIBBS on the Vibes

with JO JONES at the Drums

ZOOT SIMS AND   BREW MOORE

TENOR SAX STARS

| HOWARD McGHEE | DICK HYMAN | CLYDE LOMBARDI |
| Trumpet | Piano | Bass |

and the MILES DAVIS Quintet

with LEE KONITZ on Alto Sax and

KENNY DREW   CURLY RUSSELL

Piano   Bass

KENNY CLARKE on Drums.

PLUS AS AN ADDED ATTRACTION

the First Lady of Song

ELLA FITZGERALD

At the Jazz Corner of the World

BIRDLAND

BROADWAY, & 52nd ST. N.Y.C.   JU. 6-1368

75

THINGS TO COME

JUNE 14 — ONE WEEK ONLY

MACHITO
And His AFRO-CUBANS
CHARLIE PARKER
STAN GETZ Quintet

JUNE 21 to JUNE 30

DUKE ELLINGTON
And His World Famous Orchestra
Featuring AL HIBBLER
Plus SLIM GAILLARD

JULY 1 to JULY 18

GEORGE SHEARING
And His Quintet
Introducing LURLEAN HUNTER
Plus SLIM GAILLARD
And His All-Stars

JULY 19 to AUG. 1

DINAH WASHINGTON
With Another Great Show

STARS FOR AUGUST and SEPTEMBER

Erroll Garner	Illinois Jacquet	Lester Young
Dizzy Gillespie	Arnett Cobb	Buddy Rich
Oscar Peterson	Roy Eldridge	Flip Phillips

ALL THIS GREAT TALENT

APPEARS AT BIRDLAND
BROADWAY & 52nd ST., N.Y.C.
JU 6-1368

1951

at The JAZZ CORNER of the World

BIRDLAND
B'WAY at 52nd NEW YORK JU 6-1368

proudly presents
FOR TWO BIG WEEKS
JULY 24th thru AUGUST 6th

COUNT BASIE
ON PIANO AND ORGAN
AND HIS 17 PIECE ORCHESTRA

featuring

Paul Quinicette	Gus Johnson	Ernie Wilkins
Eddie Davis	Henry Coker	Denny Powell
Marshall Royal	Wendell Culley	Poopsie
Joe Newman	R. Jones	Jimmy Lewis
Freddy Green	T. Campbell	Jimmy Wilkins
	Bixie Crawlord	

plus

LESTER YOUNG
AND HIS QUINTET

plus

A BATTLE OF TENORS
BETWEEN
LESTER (Prez.) YOUNG & PAUL (Vice-Prez.) QUINICETTE

Listen to the BIRDLAND SHOW on WJZ 770
7 Nights a Week, Midnite to 6 A.M. featuring BOB GARRITY

at the JAZZ Corner of the World
BIRDLAND B'WAY at 52nd
NEW YORK
JU 6-1368

proudly presents

FOR ONE BIG WEEK
NOVEMBER 27 thru DECEMBER 3

DIZZY GILLESPIE

AND HIS SEXTETTE
featuring
JOE CARROLL

BUDDY DeFRANCO
AND HIS QUARTET

BILL HARRIS
and KAI WINDING GROUP
featuring

| ZOOT SIMMS | GENE RAMEY |
| DON ABNEY | ED SHAUGHANESSEY |

DON'T FORGET OUR
"JAM SESSIONS"
EVERY MONDAY NIGHT
(No cover or minimum charge during our Jam Sessions on Mondays)

Listen to the BIRDLAND SHOW on WJZ 770

1952

at the JAZZ Corner of the World
BIRDLAND B'WAY at 52nd
NEW YORK
JU 6-1368

proudly presents
THE FOLLOWING COMING ATTRACTIONS
AT NO ADVANCE IN PRICES

FOR TWO BIG WEEKS — MARCH 12-25
DIZZY GILLESPIE
AND HIS ORCHESTRA
featuring JOE CARROLL *on vocals*
ERROLL GARNER TRIO
The Amazing
BUD POWELL AND HIS TRIO

FOR ONE BIG WEEK — MARCH 26-APRIL 1
DIVINE LADY OF SONG
SARAH VAUGHAN
DIZZY GILLESPIE GARNER TRIO
AND HIS ORCHESTRA
featuring JOE CARROLL *on vocals*
TITO PUENTE & his Orchestra
(King of the Mambos)

FOR TWO BIG WEEKS — APRIL 23-MAY 6
STAN KENTON
AND HIS TWENTY THREE PIECE ORCHESTRA
THE FOUR FRESHMEN
SUNDAY AFTERNOON CONCERTS (3-6 P.M.)

FOR ONE BIG WEEK — MAY 28-JUNE 3
(THE FIRST LADY OF SONG)
ELLA FITZGERALD
BILL DAVIS TRIO
BUD POWELL TRIO

FOR TWO BIG WEEKS — JUNE 4-JUNE 17
QUEEN OF THE BLUES
Dinah Washington
BILL DAVIS TRIO
WILLIS JACKSON and HIS ORCHESTRA

DON'T FORGET OUR
"JAM SESSIONS"
EVERY MONDAY NIGHT

1953

at the JAZZ CORNER of the World
BIRDLAND
• B'WAY at 52nd
NEW YORK
JU 6-1368

proudly presents

FOR TWO BIG WEEKS
JULY 2-15
"The Great Mr. B"
BILLY ECKSTINE
LESTER YOUNG QUINTETTE
BUD POWELL TRIO

JULY 16-29 TWO BIG WEEKS
ILLINOIS JACQUET
AND HIS ALL-STARS
DIZZY GILLESPIE
AND HIS ORCHESTRA
GEORGIA CARR

AUG. 13-19
ARNETT COBB
AND HIS ORCHESTRA
WILLIS JACKSON
AND HIS ORCHESTRA
BETTY McLAURIN

AUG. 27-SEPT. 9
"The Divine Lady of Song"
SARAH VAUGHAN
DIZZY GILLESPIE
AND HIS ORCHESTRA
BUD POWELL TRIO

SEPT. 24—OCT. 7
"Queen of the Blues"
Dinah Washington
JAMES MOODY
AND HIS ORCHESTRA
BUD POWELL TRIO

FOUR BIG WEEKS
OCT. 8 - NOV. 4
ON HIS RETURN FROM EUROPE
"Modern America's Man of Music"
STAN KENTON
AND HIS ORCHESTRA
FEATURING CHRIS CONNORS

DON'T FORGET OUR
"JAM SESSIONS"
EVERY MONDAY NIGHT

Listen to the BIRDLAND SHOW on WABC 770
7 Nights a Week, Midnite to 6 A.M. featuring BOB GARRITY

at the JAZZ CORNER of the World
BIRDLAND
• B'WAY at 52nd
NEW YORK
JU 6-1368

proudly presents
AUG. 27 — SEPT. 9
Two Big Weeks
"THE DIVINE LADY OF SONG"
SARAH VAUGHAN
DIZZY GILLESPIE AND HIS ORCHESTRA
BUD POWELL TRIO

SEPT. 10 — SEPT. 16
"THE DIVINE LADY OF SONG"
SARAH VAUGHAN
SLIM GAILLARD AND HIS ALL STARS
TERRY GIBBS QUARTET

DON'T FORGET
3 Big Weeks in October
"MODERN AMERICA'S MAN OF MUSIC"
STAN KENTON
AND HIS ORCHESTRA

Listen to the BIRDLAND SHOW on WABC 770
7 Nights a Week, Midnite to 6 A.M. featuring HAL JACKSON

1954

at the JAZZ CORNER of the World

BIRDLAND

B'WAY at 52nd
NEW YORK
JU 6-1368

proudly presents

FOR THREE BIG WEEKS
MARCH 25 THRU APRIL 14

"The Divine"

S A R A H
V A U G H A N

~~~~~~~~~~~

BENNIE GREEN
AND HIS ORCHESTRA

~~~~~~~~~~~

JOHNNY SMITH QUARTET

~~~~~~~~~~~

WHEN IN FLORIDA VISIT OUR OTHER
BIRDLAND
2200 Park Avenue, Miami Beach

DON'T FORGET OUR
MONDAY NITE JAM SESSIONS

at the JAZZ CORNER of the World

BIRDLAND

B'WAY at 52nd
NEW YORK
JU 6-1368

proudly presents
FOR THREE BIG WEEKS
JULY 1st thru JULY 21st, 1954

"The Divine"

SARAH
VAUGHAN

DIZZY GILLESPIE
AND HIS ORCHESTRA

LESTER YOUNG
QUINTET

Listen to the BIRDLAND SHOW on WABC 770
7 Nights a Week Midnite to 6 A.M. featuring BOB GARRITY

Don't Forget OUR MONDAY NITE JAM SESSIONS

Poster 1 (1954)

at the JAZZ CORNER of the World

BIRDLAND

• B'WAY at 52nd
NEW YORK
JU 6-1368

PROUDLY PRESENTS

FOR THREE BIG WEEKS

QUEEN OF THE BLUES

DINAH WASHINGTON

AUG. 26th
THRU
SEPT. 15th

DIZZY **GILLESPIE** AND HIS ORCHESTRA

CHARLIE **PARKER** WITH STRINGS

BIRDLAND SHOW proudly announces that it is moving to
WINS – 1010 on your dial starting Tuesday, Sept. 7th, 1954
2 A. M. to 6 A. M. following the fabulous Allan "Moondog" Freed Show.

Don't Forget OUR MONDAY NITE JAM SESSIONS

1954

Poster 2 (1955)

at the JAZZ CORNER of the World

BIRDLAND

• B'WAY at 52nd
NEW YORK
JU 6-1368

PROUDLY PRESENTS

4 BIG WEEKS
NOV. 18th to DEC. 15th

"THE DIVINE LADY OF SONG"

SARAH VAUGHAN

— *Plus* —

NOV. 18th to DEC. 1st	DEC. 2nd to DEC. 15th
LESTER YOUNG QUINTET	**JOHNNY SMITH** QUARTET
BONNEMERE AND HIS MAMBO SEXTET	"BATTLE OF THE BARITONES" EDDIE 'Lockjaw' DAVIS vs BILLY ROOT AND THEIR QUINTET

LISTEN TO THE BIRDLAND SHOW – 6 NITES WEEKLY
OVER WINS – 1010 ON YOUR DIAL – 2 A. M. TO 6 A. M.

Don't Forget OUR MONDAY NITE JAM SESSIONS

1955

Poster 3 (1955)

at the JAZZ CORNER of the World

BIRDLAND

• B'WAY at 52nd
NEW YORK
JU 6-1368

PROUDLY PRESENTS

MAY 19th - MAY 25th	MAY 26th - JUNE 15th
THE SWINGINGEST BAND IN THE LAND **DAN TERRY** AND HIS 18 PIECE ORCHESTRA	**DIZZY GILLESPIE** AND HIS ALL STARS **STAN GETZ** AND HIS SEXTET Featuring Bob Brookmeyer
Plus "PRES" **LESTER YOUNG** AND HIS QUINTET	KING OF THE BONGOS **CANDIDO** EXTRA ATTRACTION JUNE 2nd - JUNE 15th **AL HIBBLER**

COMING JUNE 16th
STAN KENTON AND HIS 20 PC. ORCH.

LISTEN TO THE BIRDLAND SHOW NIGHTLY OVER WINS 1010 ON
YOUR DIAL – 9-10.45 P.M. – Sponsored by CRAWFORD CLOTHES

Don't Forget OUR MONDAY NITE JAM SESSIONS

1955

Poster 4 (1955)

at the JAZZ CORNER of the World

BIRDLAND

• B'WAY at 52nd
NEW YORK
JU 6-1368

PROUDLY PRESENTS

FOR 2 BIG WEEKS
JUNE 16th thru JUNE 29th

First Eastern Appearance

"MODERN AMERICA'S MAN OF MUSIC"

STAN KENTON AND HIS *NEW* ORCHESTRA

INTRODUCING

ANN RICHARDS

Plus

20 Of The World's Most Outstanding Instrumentalists

Sensational New Capitol Recording Artists

THE MIL-COMBO
— *NO INCREASE IN PRICES* —

COMING JUNE 30th
COUNT BASIE AND HIS 16 PC. ORCH.

LISTEN TO THE BIRDLAND SHOW NIGHTLY OVER WINS 1010 ON
YOUR DIAL – 9-10.45 P.M.

Don't Forget OUR MONDAY NITE JAM SESSIONS

1955

1955

1955

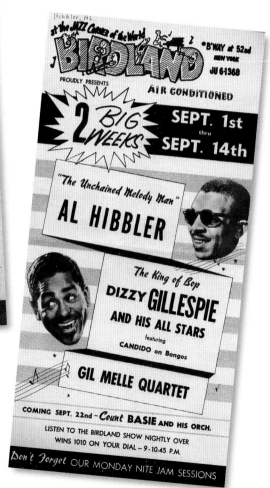

1955

1955

1956

at the JAZZ Corner of the World
BIRDLAND
• B'WAY at 52nd
NEW YORK
JU 6-7333

PROUDLY PRESENTS

MARCH 29th to APRIL 18th

"QUEEN OF THE BLUES"
DINAH
WASHINGTON

JOHNNY	AL
SMITH	**BELLETTO**
QUARTET	SEXTET

COMING APRIL 19th — CARMEN McRAE
COMING MAY 3rd — BUD POWELL

LISTEN TO THE BIRDLAND SHOW NIGHTLY
OVER WINS 1010 ON YOUR DIAL — 9-10:45 P.M.

1956

84

at the JAZZ Corner of the World
BIRDLAND
• B'WAY at 52nd
NEW YORK
JU 6-1368

PROUDLY PRESENTS

FOR 2 BIG WEEKS!

"the Count of Swing"...
Count Basie
AND HIS 16 PIECE ORCHESTRA

FEATURING
JOE WILLIAMS ON VOCALS

JUNE
7
thru
JUNE
20

HENRY COKER	WENDELL CULLEY	FREDDIE GREEN
BILL HUGHES	RENNALDO JONES	THAD JONES
CHARLES FOWLKES	SONNY PAYNE	FRANK FOSTER
JOE NEWMAN	BENNIE POWELL	MARSHALL ROYAL
FRANK WESS	ED JONES	BILL GRAHAM

—— Plus ——

TERRY GIBBS QUARTET

COMING JUNE 21st
JERI SOUTHERN

LISTEN TO THE BIRDLAND SHOW NIGHTLY OVER
WINS 1010 ON YOUR DIAL — 9-10:45 P.M.

1956

1956

1956

NOV. 8th to NOV. 21st

DUKE ELLINGTON

AND HIS WORLD FAMOUS ORCHESTRA

•

NORM AMADIO QUARTET

NOV. 22nd to DEC. 5th

DIZZY GILLESPIE

AND HIS 16 PIECE ORCHESTRA

•

HORACE SILVER QUINTET

DECEMBER 6th

BASIE'S BACK HOME

Don't Forget OUR MONDAY NITE JAM SESSIONS

1956

1957

at the JAZZ Corner of the World

BIRDLAND

● B'WAY at 52nd
NEW YORK

JU 6-7333

One Week Only
JAN. 3rd — JAN. 9th
CHRIS CONNOR

MODERN JAZZ QUARTET
**JOHN LEWIS — MILT JACKSON
PERCY HEATH — CONNIE KAY**

LES MODES QUINTET
WITH
CHARLIE ROUSE and JULIUS WATKINS

JAN. 10th — JAN. 23rd
MORGANA KING

BUDDY DE FRANCO
AND HIS QUINTET

CHARLIE MINGUS
AND HIS QUARTET

Don't Forget OUR MONDAY NITE JAM SESSIONS

1957

at the JAZZ Corner of the World

BIRDLAND

● B'WAY at 52nd
NEW YORK

JU 6-7333

JAN. 24th — FEB. 6th
AL HIBBLER

"THE AMAZING"
BUD POWELL TRIO

JOHNNY SMITH QUARTET

One Week Only
FEB. 7th — FEB. 13th
COUNT BASIE
**AND HIS ORCHESTRA
WITH JOE WILLIAMS**

JOHNNY SMITH QUARTET

Opening
FEB. 14th — CARMEN McRAE

Don't Forget OUR MONDAY NITE JAM SESSIONS

1957

1957

1957

1957

1958

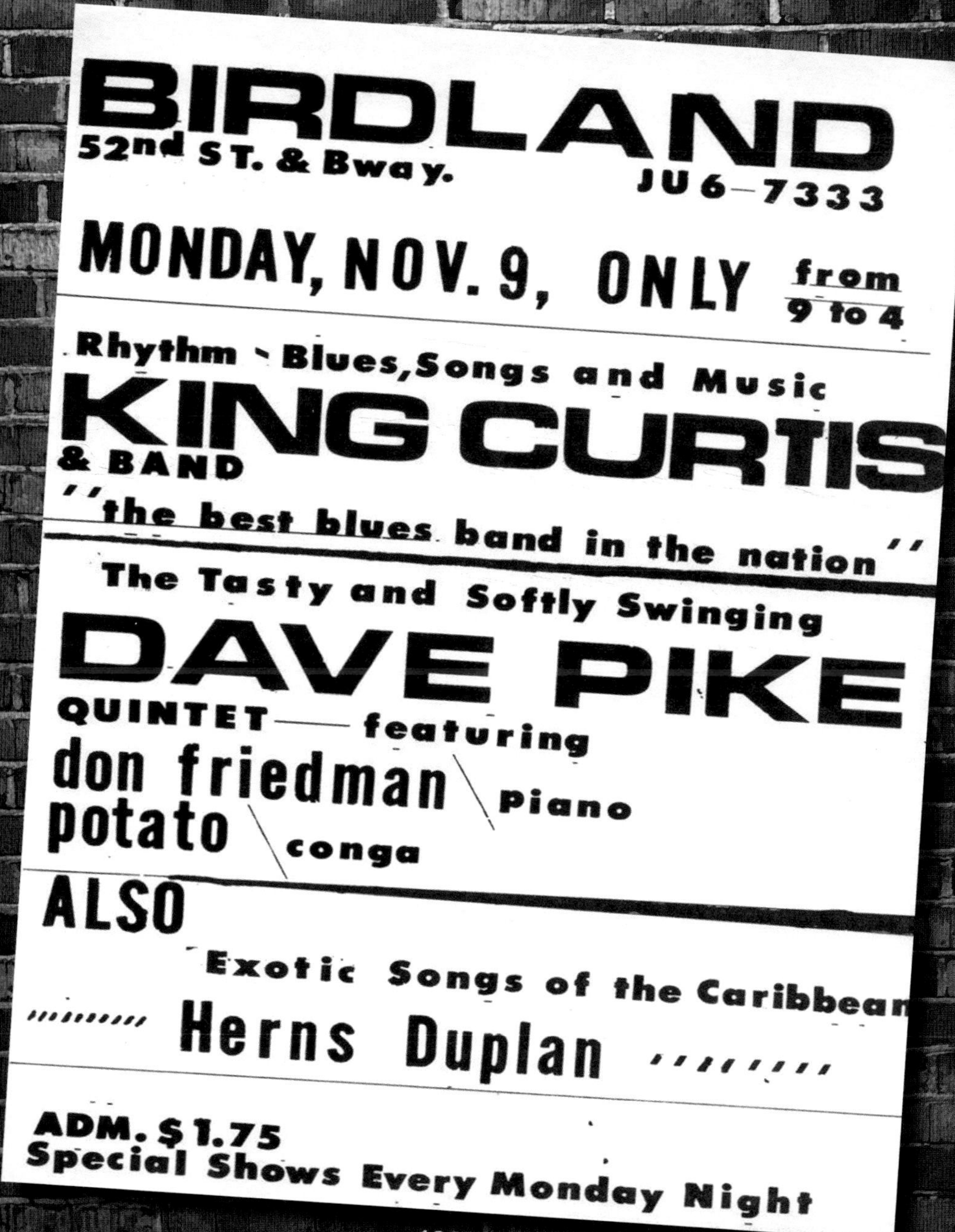

BIRDLAND
52nd ST. & Bway.   JU 6-7333

MONDAY, NOV. 9, ONLY   from 9 to 4

Rhythm - Blues, Songs and Music
KING CURTIS
& BAND
"the best blues band in the nation"

The Tasty and Softly Swinging
DAVE PIKE
QUINTET —— featuring
don friedman \ Piano
potato \ conga

ALSO
Exotic Songs of the Caribbean
'''''' Herns Duplan ''''''''

ADM. $1.75
Special Shows Every Monday Night

1963

89

CHAPTER SIX

BIRDLAND

LIVE RECORDINGS

LENNIE TRISTANO QUINTET
LIVE AT BIRDLAND 1949

Includes
solo piano
selections

Charlie Parker & Dizzy Gillespie
Complete Live at BIRDLAND

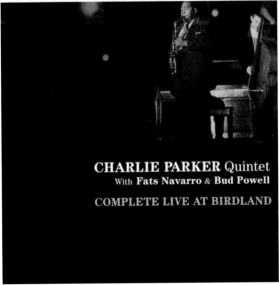

CHARLIE PARKER Quintet
With Fats Navarro & Bud Powell

COMPLETE LIVE AT BIRDLAND

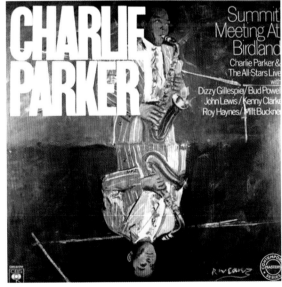

CHARLIE PARKER

Summit
Meeting At
Birdland
Charlie Parker &
The All-Stars Live
with
Dizzy Gillespie / Bud Powell
John Lewis / Kenny Clarke
Roy Haynes / Milt Buckner

THE ENCHANTING ELLA FITZGERALD

LIVE AT BIRDLAND 1950-1952

MILES DAVIS - BIRDLAND DAYS

Featuring STAN GETZ

FRESH SOUND RECORDS

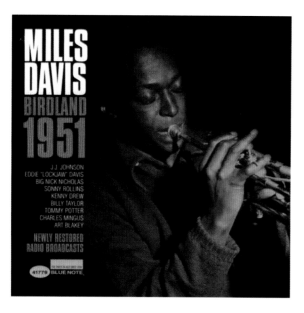

MILES DAVIS

BIRDLAND 1951

J.J. JOHNSON
EDDIE "LOCKJAW" DAVIS
BIG NICK NICHOLAS
SONNY ROLLINS
KENNY DREW
BILLY TAYLOR
TOMMY POTTER
CHARLES MINGUS
ART BLAKEY

NEWLY RESTORED
RADIO BROADCASTS

41779 BLUE NOTE

TRANE'S FIRST RIDE 1951
John Coltrane
FIRST BROADCASTS
Never Available Before

• CONGO BLUES
• NIGHT IN TUNISIA
• YESTERDAYS
• BIRK'S WORKS
• GOOD BAIT
• I CAN'T GET STARTED
• BIRK'S WORKS (AIR CHECK)
• JUMPING WITH SYMPHONY !

OBERON 1500

THE METRONOME SERIES

SLIM GAILLARD
and His Friends

Slim Gaillard at Birdland 1951

BEN WEBSTER

BIRDLAND
1952

JAZZ ANTHOLOGY

Lester Young

Live at Birdland

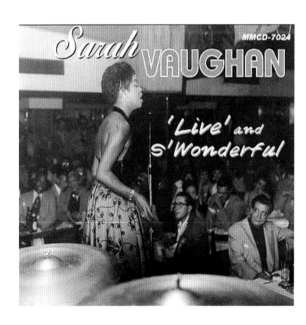

Sarah VAUGHAN

MMCD-7024

'Live' and S'Wonderful

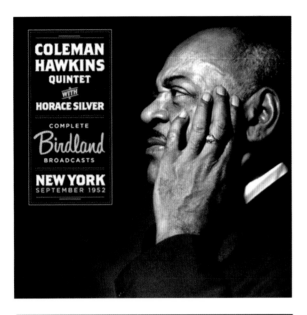

COLEMAN
HAWKINS
QUINTET
WITH
HORACE SILVER
COMPLETE
Birdland
BROADCASTS
NEW YORK
SEPTEMBER 1952

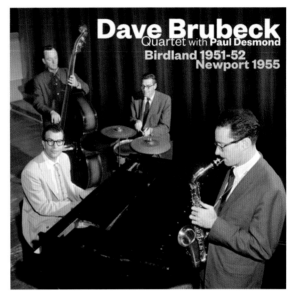

Dave Brubeck
Quartet with Paul Desmond
Birdland 1951-52
Newport 1955

STAN
GETZ
QUINTET

FEATURING
JIMMY
RANEY

BIRDLAND
SESSIONS 1952

Charles Mingus
Horace Silver
Duke Jordan
Connie Kay
Gene Ramey
Phil Brown

The Slide Hampton Octet

Featuring Freddie Hubbard · George Coleman · Jay Cameron

Somethin' Sanctified · Sister Salvation · Live at Birdland

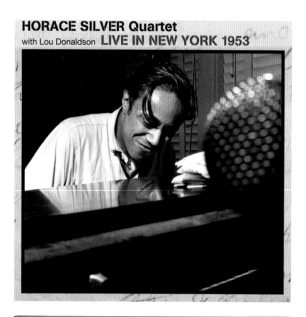

HORACE SILVER Quartet
with Lou Donaldson LIVE IN NEW YORK 1953

COUNT BASIE
AIR SHOTS BIRDLAND
January 1953
VOLUME ONE

unique jazz

AT BIRDLAND

気心知れたアル・コーンとの熱演で、
世界初出の1952年の瑞々しいズート
のライブ。
CD／LP共に限定99枚シリアル番号入り。

アット・バードランド／ズート・シムズ

HISTORICAL SERIES

Lester visits Basie

COUNT BASIE
AIR SHOTS BIRDLAND
January 1953
VOLUME TWO

unique jazz

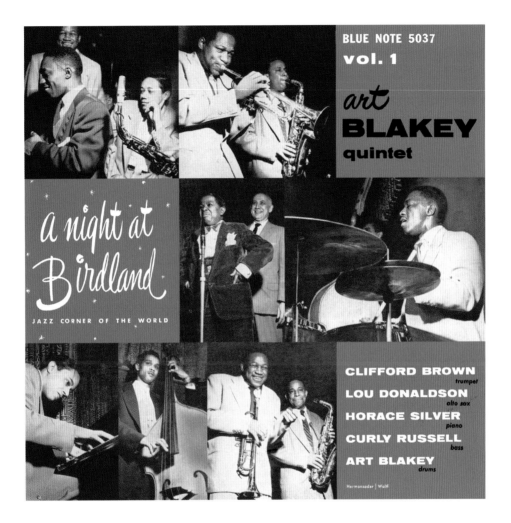

Recorded at Birdland on February 21, 1954. This recording made jazz history by being the first of its kind ever to be recorded at a live venue, using a record label's equipment. This album showcased the birth of hard bop and set up the framework for Art Blakey's next musical adventure—the Jazz Messengers.

The displayed photographic images show the band members listed on the front cover. The center image is of emcee Pee Wee Marquette and the manager, Oscar Goodstein. There is also a Vol. 2 record.

JAZZ BAND
COMPACT CLASSICS
EBCD 2135-2

Stan Kenton

The 1950's Birdland Broadcasts

COOL BLUE

TENOR BATTLE AT BIRDLAND

SONNY STITT & EDDIE DAVIS

A SERIES LIVE FROM THE VAULTS

MMCD-9002

Stan KENTON

'Live' Birdland Encores

DIGITALLY REMASTERED AT THE ARCHIVES

FRIEDRICH GULDA AND HIS SEXTET AT BIRDLAND

Featuring
Idrees Sulieman
Jimmy Cleveland
Phil Woods
Seldon Powell
Aaron Bell
Nick Stabulas

THE MODERN JAZZ QUARTET

at Birdland

LN 3118

EPIC

W!LD BILL DAVIS AT BIRDLAND

WILD BILL DAVIS

Echoes of an Era

BIRDLAND ALL STARS AT CARNEGIE HALL

SARAH VAUGHAN

CHARLIE PARKER

STAN GETZ

BILLIE HOLIDAY

LESTER YOUNG

COUNT BASIE

Dizzy Gillespie Big Band

GROOVIN' HIGH

Live at Birdland, New York City

An Afternoon at Birdland

with KAI WINDING and J. J. JOHNSON

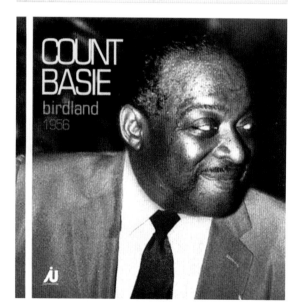

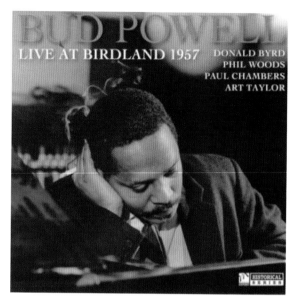

MAYNARD FERGUSON
AND HIS
BIRDLAND
DREAM BAND

Arrangements by BILL HOLMAN, BOB BROOKMEYER
MARTY PAICH, JIMMY GIUFFRE, JOHNNY MANDEL
MANNY ALBAM, ERNIE WILKINS and WILLIE MAIDEN

Featuring NICK TRAVIS, AL COHN
HERB GELLER, JIMMY CLEVELAND
BUDD JOHNSON and HANK JONES

In 1956, Maynard Ferguson led the Birdland Dream Band, a fourteen-piece big band assembled for the Birdland jazz club in New York City. This was one of the most exciting bands that Maynard ever led, opening at Birdland on August 30, 1956. Although they were short lived, this band became the core of Maynard's performing band for the next nine years. This album was recorded in the studio.

A NEW ROULETTE SOUND **DYNAMIC STEREO** ROULETTE SR 52022

Hank Mobley   Billy Root
Curtis Fuller   Lee Morgan

*another
monday
night
at
birdland*

ROULETTE
BIRDLAND SERIES

JAZZ OFF THE AIR VOL. 5

BUDDY RICH
WITH SONNY CRISS, KENNY DREW
OLE HANSEN AND PHIL LESHIN
THE CINCH

SPOTLITE SPJ 149   Birdland 1958

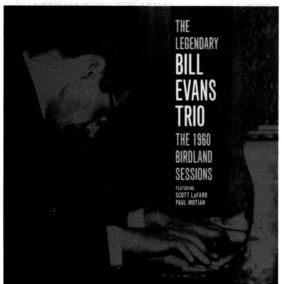

THE
LEGENDARY
**BILL
EVANS
TRIO**

THE 1960
BIRDLAND
SESSIONS

FEATURING
SCOTT LaFARO
PAUL MOTIAN

FRESH SOUND RECORDS

STAN GETZ
QUARTET
AT BIRDLAND 1961
Featuring STEVE KUHN
JIMMY GARRISON & ROY HAYNES

*These previously unreleased 1961 performances
recorded live at Birdland, show Getz bringing
his tenor saxophone mastery to new heights in
a truly stunning comeback.*

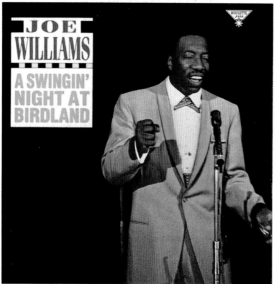

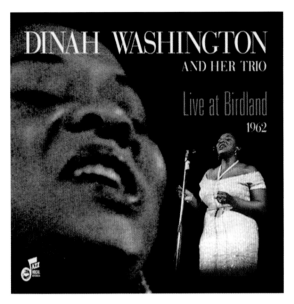

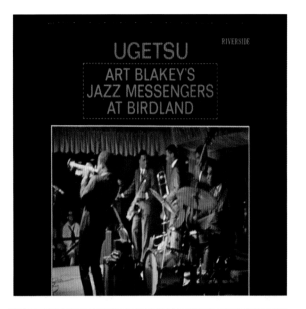

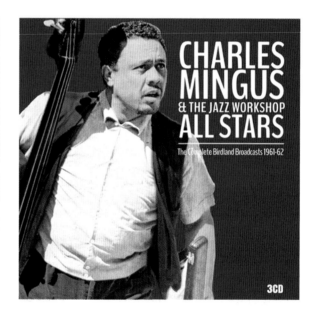

CHAPTER SEVEN

BIRDLAND

MEMORABILIA

Birdland postcard

BIRDLAND

NEW YORK AND

BROADWAY'S OLDEST

JAZZ CLUB

"THE DIVINE LADY OF SONG"
SARAH VAUGHAN
BIRDLAND

Birdland, 12 years old, has the distinction of being Broadway's Oldest Jazz Club. Birdland is established thruout the world today as America's foremost jazz rendezvous. It has truly become an institution. Aptly subtitled, "at the Jazz Corner of the World", Birdland is recognized all over the globe. Leading music publications in France, Italy, Sweden, England, Germany, Japan, Argentina, Australia, India and South Africa have written numerous feature stories on Birdland and its unique place in modern music.

Birdland, to the devotees of the ultra modern in music is home. Birdland is not what the word implies. It is a place of "relaxed" listening. It is the tempo of what is known in the vernacular as the cool sound, the frantic mood, the gone riff. It is a place of expression for the music of yesterday, today, tomorrow and always — for music never dies.

At Birdland every night, new musical sounds are in a constant state of creation. Some of these creations later become classics. Birdland customers have heard chords, notes & tones never before achieved, many of them unbelievable in quality and originality. One must go there to hear and believe.

Many so called "long hair listeners" come the first time as unbelievers to scoff and ridicule — but go away bedazzled and amazed at the sincerity of the performers, the beauty of their renditions, their dexterity and artistry. Birdland is the home of all good modern expressions, where you hear music from the instrumental voice of Sarah Vaughan to the magnificent transpositions of a George Shearing or perhaps the thumping excitement of a Count Basie.

Acoustically Birdland is the most perfect in the United States — it is Hi-Fi in motion, sans record and phonograph . . .

Many serious students of music who sit quietly in the Bull-pen absorbing the cool sounds have correctly termed Birdland a Music Hall rather than a nightclub . . .

An average of 5,000 people visit the Jive-Inn every single week. Since it opened Dec. 15th, 1949, more than three million eight hundred thousand people from all over the world have thrilled to the cool musical sounds therein . . .

Many famous names visit the club nightly. Some of Birdland's celebrated regulars whom you are liable to rub shoulders with include Doris Duke, Gary Cooper, Marilyn Monroe, Jane Russell, Ava Gardner, Frank Sinatra, Janis Paige, Joe Louis, Jackie Gleason, Sid Caesar, Red Buttons, Red Skelton, etc.

Things You Never Knew About Birdland...

Birdland spends more money per year for musicians than the Philharmonic Orchestra . . .

Before sailors and crew even go to their hotels (when foreign ships dock in New York) they "make it" to Birdland . . .

Birdland is the mecca of musicians from all over the world. Many foreign musicians, who cannot express themselves in English frequently sit in and express themselves in music . . .

Birdland attracts more college professors than any other night club in the country. Professors who teach music at various metropolitan colleges often bring their entire classes to Birdland on field trips. Some colleges are: New York University, Columbia, New York School of Music, Juilliard School of Music, etc. . . .

The Lullaby of Birdland Story...

Lullaby of Birdland, the biggest jazz pop standard to come out in the last ten years, is the theme of song of Birdland. The tune, only nine years old was written by George Shearing, who frequently appears at Birdland. Shearing has rendered thousands of lullaby at Birdland for he was among the first to play the room 12 years ago. There are more than 100 records out on it. It sells consistently well in all its versions throughout the United States, England, Germany, France and even Japan. Lullaby of Birdland is not only the trademark of Birdland — it is the theme heard most often in jazz clubs and music rooms all over the globe. The lyrics have been translated into German, French, Italian, Spanish and Swedish.

One of RCA Victor's current best selling albums is an unusual album that has twelve interpretations of Lullaby of Birdland by twelve different outstanding jazz groups.

Birdland brochure page 3

Milton Berle — Mr. TV clowning with Slim Gaillard, the zany musical jester at Birdland

Benny Goodman, the King of Swing himself, entertains a party of international celebrities at Birdland — among them Jackie Coogan, Duke Ellington and Don Budge

WORld famed commentator Walter Winchell, heard over more than 600 stations, entertains an audience of two — Duke Ellington and Yul Brynner in a cozy Birdland Corner

Comedian Henny Youngman gets carried away by Birdland atmosphere and gives song star Billy Eckstine a lesson in crooning

Gary Cooper lets out with his million dollar smile at the nightly hip-to-do at Birdland

Henry Fonda, who is very Fonda Flats and Fugues as played at Birdland

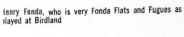

Peter Lawford and his wife having kicks for a few ticks at Birdland after a night on the town

Two celebrated regulars at the mecca for musicians Phil Harris and Alice Faye

Birdland brochure page 4

Dean Martin and Jerry Lewis in a gay happy mood listening to the cool sounds at the Jazz Corner of the World

Marlon Brando is a familiar figure on the Birdland scene where he frequently sits in on Bongos. Here he is seen with blues stylist Dinah Washington and America's top folk singer Harry Belafonte who got his start at Birdland ten years ago in the very first show

Paul Whiteman, King of Jazz who pioneered the pop trend, on one of his frequent visits to Birdland with modernist Stan Kenton

Jackie Cooper and Janis Paige at Birdland chuckling over the merry musical antics of Dizzy Gillespie

Duke Ellington — composer-conductor steps from the podium to greet two well known regulars Skitch Henderson and Faye Emerson

Birdland brochure page 5

Dean Martin & Jerry Lewis

Sammy Davis Jr.

Sammy Davis Jr. — Mr. Talent gets carried away and beats out a few hot licks on the hides

Jackie Cooper & Janis Paige

Henry Fonda

Birdland souvenir photo folder

on broadway at 52nd street

where the "bill" is always low!

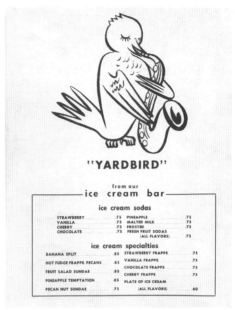

"YARDBIRD"

from our
ice cream bar

ice cream sodas

STRAWBERRY	.75	PINEAPPLE	.75
VANILLA	.75	MALTED MILK	.75
CHERRY	.75	FROSTED	.75
CHOCOLATE	.75	FRESH FRUIT SODAS	
		(ALL FLAVORS)	.75

ice cream specialties

BANANA SPLIT	.85	STRAWBERRY FRAPPE	.75
HOT FUDGE FRAPPE, PECANS	.85	VANILLA FRAPPE	.75
FRUIT SALAD SUNDAE	.85	CHOCOLATE FRAPPE	.75
PINEAPPLE TEMPTATION	.85	CHERRY FRAPPE	.75
PECAN NUT SUNDAE	.75	PLATE OF ICE CREAM	
		(ALL FLAVORS)	.60

from our kitchen

appetizers

FRUIT COCKTAIL	.30
TOMATO JUICE	.30
ORANGE JUICE	.30
GRAPEFRUIT JUICE	.30
PINEAPPLE JUICE	.30
CHICKEN BROTH WITH RICE	.30

cold sandwiches

VIRGINIA HAM	.95
TURKEY	.95
HAMBURGER	.75
BACON AND TOMATO	.85
LETTUCE AND TOMATO	.75
CLUB SANDWICH	1.50
HAM AND CHEESE	1.10
CHEESE	.75

beverages

COFFEE	.25
TEA	.25
MILK	.30
ICED COFFEE	.30
ICED TEA	.30

southern fried chicken
FRENCH FRIED POTATOES
COLE SLAW
ROLLS AND BUTTER
$1.75

barbecue ribs
FRENCH FRIED POTATOES
COLE SLAW
ROLLS AND BUTTER
$1.75

ham steak
PINEAPPLE RINGS
FRENCH FRIED POTATOES
COLE SLAW AND VEGETABLE
ROLLS AND BUTTER
$1.75

hot ham sandwich
FRENCH FRIED POTATOES
VEGETABLE
$1.65

hot turkey sandwich
FRENCH FRIED POTATOES
COLE SLAW
$1.65

chopped steak
FRENCH FRIED POTATOES
COLE SLAW AND VEGETABLE
ROLLS AND BUTTER
$1.75

barbecue chicken
FRENCH FRIED POTATOES
COLE SLAW AND VEGETABLE
ROLLS AND BUTTER
$1.75

barbecue beef steak
FRENCH FRIED POTATOES
COLE SLAW AND VEGETABLE
ROLLS AND BUTTER
$1.95

crispy fried giblets .65

french fried potatoes .50

french fried onion rings .50

wines and liquors

moscow mule .95
A DRINK WITH A "KICK"

cocktails

MARTINI	.75
BRONX	.75
ORANGE BLOSSOM	.75
MANHATTAN	.75
DUBONNET	.75
JACK ROSE	.75
BACARDI	.75
CLOVER CLUB	.75
DAIQUIRI	.75
PINK LADY	.75
OLD FASHIONED	.75
ALEXANDER WITH GIN	.85
SAZARAC	.85
ST. JAMES	.95
FROZEN DAIQUIRI	.85
CHAMPAGNE	1.00
SIDE CAR	1.00
STINGER	1.00
ALEXANDER WITH BRANDY	1.00

mixed drinks

ORANGE OR LEMONADE	.75
TOM COLLINS	.75
JOHN COLLINS	.75
WHISKEY SOUR	.75
RUM COLLINS	.75
CUBA LIBRE	.75
RUM AND COCO COLA	.75
WARD "8"	.80
CLARET LEMONADE	.75
SHERRY FLIP	.85
SINGAPORE SLING	1.00
PLANTER'S PUNCH	1.00
MINT JULEP	1.25
ZOMBIE	1.75

snow cloud $1.10
WILL STAND YOU
ON YOUR HEAD

gin

DRY GIN	.75
SLOE GIN	.75
SLOE GIN FIZZ	.75
GIN HIGHBALL	.75
GIN RICKEY	.75
GIN FIZZ	.75
SLOE GIN RICKEY	.75
SILVER FIZZ	.85
GOLDEN FIZZ	.85

scotch

BLACK & WHITE	.85
WHITE HORSE	.85
DEWAR'S WHITE LABEL	.85
CUTTY SARK	.85
TEACHERS	.85
BALLANTINE	.85
JOHNNY WALKER RED LABEL	.85
VAT 69	.85
HAIG & HAIG 5 STAR	.85
GRAND MACNISH	.85
USHER'S GREEN STRIPE	.85
OLD ANGUS	.85
GILBEY'S SPEY ROYAL	.85
KING WILLIAM IV	.85
BLACK & WHITE DELUXE	.95
HAIG & HAIG PINCH	.95
DEWAR'S VICTORIA VAT	.95
JOHNNY WALKER BLACK LABEL	.95
USHER'S LIQUEUR	.95
HIGHLAND NECTAR	.95
HOUSE OF LORDS	.95
MARTIN'S V. V. O.	.95
HIGHLAND QUEEN	.95
J. & B.	.95
KING'S RANSOM	.95

cognac

APPLEJACK PONIES	.75
HENNESSY 3 STAR	.95
BISQUIT DUBOUCHE	.95
MONNEY 3 STAR	.95
HINE 3 STAR	.95
MARTELL 3 STAR	.95
COURVOISIER	.95
OTARD 3 STAR	.95
REMY MARTIN 3 STAR	.95
REMY MARTIN V. S. E. P.	1.25

FOR IMPORTED AND DOMESTIC

wines and champagne

ASK FOR THE HEAD WAITER

rye

SCHENLEY RESERVE	.75
WILSON	.75
MT. VERNON	.75
CARSTAIR'S WHITE SEAL	.75
IMPERIAL	.75
CALVERT RESERVE	.75
PARK & TILFORD RESERVE	.75
FOUR ROSES	.75
LORD CALVERT	.75
PARK & TILFORD PRIVATE STOCK	.75
OLD OVERHOLT (BONDED)	.85
CANADIAN CLUB	.85
SEAGRAM'S V.O.	.85
HARWOOD'S	.85
DUNBAR	.85

bourbon

THREE FEATHERS V. S. R.	.75
BOURBON DE LUXE	.75
WALKER'S DE LUXE	.75
I. W. HARPER	.85
OLD GRANDAD	.85
OLD TAYLOR	.85
OLD FORESTER	.85
KENTUCKY TAVERN	.85

liqueurs

ANISETTE PONIES	.85
CREME DE CACAO	.85
CREME DE MENTHE (GREEN)	.85
CREME DE MENTHE (WHITE)	.85
APRICOT OR CHERRY	.85
PEACH OR BLACKBERRY	.85
TRIPLE SEC	.85
B. & B. (D. O. M.)	.95
BENEDICTINE (D. O. M.)	.95
DRAMBUIE	.95
CHERRY HEERING	1.10
VODKA	.95
SOUTHERN COMFORT	.95

beer and ale

BALLANTINE'S ALE	.75
PABST BLUE RIBBON	.75
SCHLITZ	.75
RHEINGOLD	.75
BUDWEISER	.75
SCHAEFFER	.75

Birdland menu

Birdland Stars of '57 souvenir program

Sarah Vaughan & Billy Eckstine

Count Basie

Pee Wee Marquette & Slim Gaillard

Count Basie & Sarah Vaughan

IF YOU WISH TO RECEIVE ADVANCE NEWS ON ALL FUTURE "BIRDLAND PRESENTS" SHOWS, PLEASE FILL OUT COUPON BELOW, OR REASONABLE FACSIMILE AND MAIL TO

BIRDLAND PRESENTS INC.
1619 BROADWAY
NEW YORK, N. Y.

NAME _____

STREET & NUMBER _____

CITY & STATE _____

AUDITORIUM WHICH YOU LAST PATRONIZED TO SEE THESE SHOWS _____

ADDITIONAL COPIES OF "BIRDLAND PRESENTS" SOUVENIR PROGRAMS MAY BE OBTAINED BY MAILING ONE DOLLAR TO PROGRAM PUB. CO.,

PROGRAM

BUD POWELL

PHINEAS NEWBORN JR.

CHET BAKER

LESTER YOUNG

ZOOT SIMS

JERI SOUTHERN

COUNT BASIE
featuring
JOE WILLIAMS

INTERMISSION

TERRY GIBBS QUARTETTE
featuring
TERRY POLLARD

JIMMY JONES – ROY HAYNES – RICHARD DAVIS

SELDON POWELL

ROLF KUHN

SARAH VAUGHAN

BILLY ECKSTINE

Program subject to change

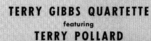

CHET BAKER

SO WHAT! THEY BREAK THAT BARRIER EVERY NOTE AT BIRDLAND

IS THIS THE PLACE THAT'S OUT OF THIS WORLD?

WHAT SPECIES OF BIRD DO YOU KEEP IN THERE?

ROLF KUHN

SELDON POWELL

LESTER YOUNG

ZOOT SIMS

Birdland swizzle sticks and bakelite ashtray

Birdland, jazz corner of world, gives visiting drummers use of its spectacular GRETSCH green and gold set

at the JAZZ CORNER of the World
BIRDLAND

Jo Jones
Mel Lewis
Sonny Payne
Charlie Persip
Max Roach
Art Taylor

Birdland MC Pee Wee Marquette, Birdland Mgr. Oscar Goodstein

Emcee Pee Wee Marquette and Birdland
manager Oscar Goodstein

Birdland, New York
(Thursday, July 6)

Capacity, 273. Price policy, $2 minimum, except Monday (jazz session) nights. Music continuous from 9 to 4. Owner-operators, Irving Levy and Morris Primack. Booking policy, non-exclusive. Estimated budget this show, $2,300. Estimated budget last show, $2,500.

The new show at Birdland is up to here in saxophones.

The feature is alto saxist Charlie Parker, backed by a hybrid but eminently pleasant ork of three violins, viol, cello, oboe and harp, and an orthodox piano-bass-drums rhythm section. This wedding of traditional chamber music with modern jazz stems from a Mercury Records album, *Parker With Strings*, the favorable response to which apparently encouraged Parker to try the same thing live. The repertory, so far, is limited to the album selections—standards like *April in Paris, I Didn't Know What Time It Was, Just Friends, If I Should Lose You*, etc. The arrangements are formal, polite and unpretentious, calculated to furnish the virtuoso altoist with a rich-textured but unobtrusive backdrop for his sax flights. His playing, for the most part, is much simpler, restrained and observant of the written melodies than has been his wont. It is a new phase for Parker, who having established himself as a master of the most intricate and inventive saxophone playing ever, now goes completely and ultimately "cool," relying on purity and simplicity of expression and utter chasteness of tone and attack. The fans ate it up, but it's a fair guess Parker will have to expand and vary his program if he hopes to sustain audience interest after the novelty wears off. More and different arrangements, a vocalist, a few unvarnished, swinging numbers both with the chamber group and solo with the rhythm section should be added.

The other attractions are tenor saxist Gene Ammon's small jump band and tenor saxist Stan Getz's bop quartet. The Ammons combo fared satisfactorily when they essayed jump tunes featuring unison riffs, died on slow, sour-sounding ballads. Bright spot is tenor Sonny Stitt, a brilliant bopper who "cut" leader Ammons to the huge delight of the illuminati in the bleachers. Getz is so cool, nonchalant and disinterested that only the faithful can restrain yawns.

at the JAZZ CORNER of the World

BIRDLAND

proudly presents a few of the great
JAZZ artists who will appear
in 1958

COUNT BASIE
STAN GETZ
MILES DAVIS
DIZZY GILLESPIE
JERI SOUTHERN
AL HIBBLER
STAN KENTON
BUD POWELL
JOHNNY SMITH
SARAH VAUGHAN
JOHNNY RICHARDS
JOE WILLIAMS

BIRDLAND   52nd Street & Broadway, New York, N. Y.
JUdson 6-7333

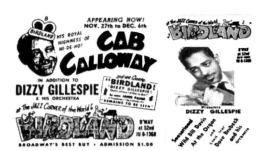

APPEARING NOW!
NOV. 27th to DEC. 6th

HIS ROYAL
HIGHNESS OF
HI-DE-HO!

CAB CALLOWAY

IN ADDITION TO
DIZZY GILLESPIE
& HIS ORCHESTRA

"BIRDLAND"
DIZZY GILLESPIE
REMAINS TO BE SEEN

at the JAZZ CORNER of the World

BIRDLAND

B'WAY at 52nd
JU 6-1368

BROADWAY'S BEST BUY · ADMISSION $1.00

Sensational
Wild Bill Davis
At the Organ

BIRDLAND

Presents
DIZZY GILLESPIE

Dave Brubeck
and his
Orchestra

PHONE: WH 4-1011

HOUSE OF ENG
AND
CONFUCIUS LOUNGE

106 E. WALTON PLACE
CHICAGO, ILL.

December 6th to 26th

► Direct from his Triumphant ◄
European Tour

COUNT

BASIE

and his 16 pc. orchestra

featuring **JOE WILLIAMS**

PHINEAS NEWBORN Quartet

BiRDLAND

52nd ST. and BROADWAY
JUdson 6-7333

THE JAZZ CORNER OF THE WORLD

...and **BIRDLAND** *salutes*

THE GREAT ARTISTS WHO
HAVE OVER THE PAST
10 YEARS MADE IT

*"THE JAZZ CORNER OF
THE WORLD"*

COUNT BASIE	STAN GETZ
MAYNARD FERGUSON	DUKE ELLINGTON
SARAH VAUGHAN	DINAH WASHINGTON
STAN KENTON	BUDDY RICH
J. J. JOHNSON	DAVE BRUBECK
KAI WINDING	HORACE SILVER
GEORGE SHEARING	BUD POWELL
DIZZY GILLESPIE	CHARLIE MINGUS
"CANNONBALL" ADDERLEY	MAX ROACH
TONY SCOTT	CHICO HAMILTON
JIMMY GUIFFRE	WOODY HERMAN
HARRY EDISON	ELLA FITZGERALD
PHINEAS NEWBORN JR.	CHRIS CONNOR
ERROL GARNER	SLIM GAILLARD
DAKOTA STATON	ILLOIS JACQUET
ARNETT COBB	JOHNNY SMITH
TERRY GIBBS	MERCER ELLINGTON
JOHNNY RICHARDS	OSCAR PETTIFORD
ART BLAKEY	BOB BROOKMEYER

AND "A MEMORIAL SALUTE TO THE JAZZ IMMORTALS

CLIFFORD BROWN   **LESTER YOUNG**
FATS NAVARRO   **CHARLIE PARKER**   **ART TATUM**

BIRDLAND
52nd STREET and BROADWAY

125

My personal autographed Birdland menu. All the autographs are from one evening at Birdland in 1952. Left side, bottom: Dizzy Gillespie and George Shearing. Left side, top: Al McKibbon, Oscar Peterson, and Chuck Wayne. Right side, top: Milt Jackson and Joe Carroll. Right side, bottom: Art Blakey.

SOURCES

During my research for this book I drew from many secondary and primary sources, such as *Time* magazine; *DownBeat* magazine; the *New York Times*; the *African-American* newspaper; *Wail: The Life of Bud Powell*, by Peter Pullman; *Let's Get to the Nitty Gritty: The Autobiography of Horace Silver*; *Lullaby of Birdland: The Autobiography of George Shearing*; *Bird: The Life and Music of Charlie Parker*, by Chuck Haddix; and *Godfather of the Music Business: Morris Levy*, by Richard Carlin. I also obtained helpful information from the Library of Congress and author / jazz bassist Bill Crow, who graciously allowed me to utilize material from his wonderful book *From Broadway to Birdland*.

I am also appreciative to all the individuals who have allowed me to use the historical Birdland photographs and handbills in this book. All of their names are listed in the photo credits section of this book.

In the memorabilia section of this book, most of the displayed items are part of my personal collection of Birdland memorabilia.

I would also like to thank all the record companies that produced albums (over fifty) from tapes or acetates received from live recordings performed at Birdland over its historic fifteen-year run, and for the use of the album covers used in this book.

THE AUTHOR

Leo T. Sullivan (saxophonist, flutist, composer, webmaster) has worked professionally for over forty years and has played on numerous CDs with various artists, having also recorded soundtracks for major television shows. Leo has played with the Manhattan Transfer, Johnny Mathis, Rosemary Clooney, the Temptations, Toni Tennille, Charo, Don Rickles, Carl Fontana, Bob Newhart, and the Osmond Brothers, just to name a few. In recent years, Leo has been involved in developing over sixty-five jazz websites and has done so out of pocket and for nonprofit. You can view the jazz websites at www.jazzwebsites.org.